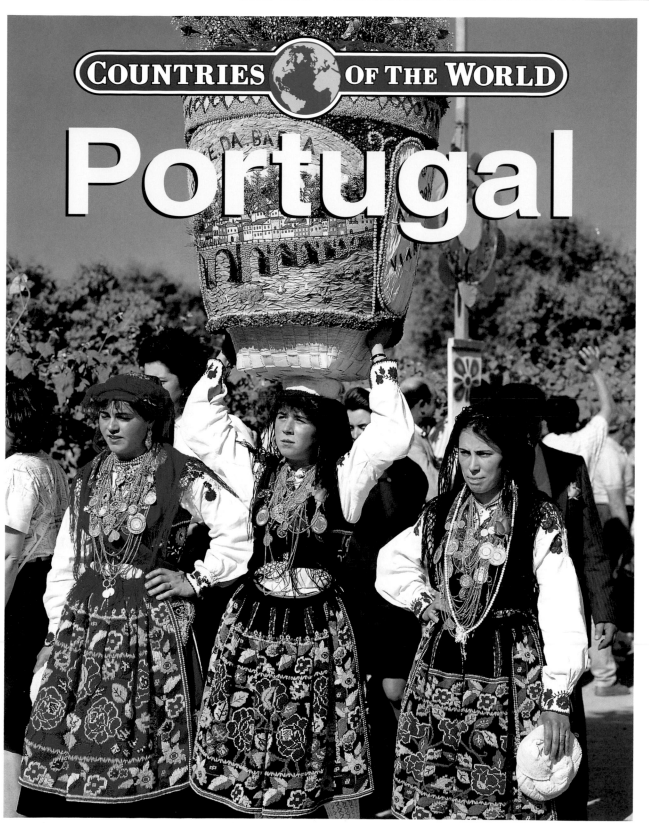

COUNTRIES OF THE WORLD

Portugal

Gareth Stevens Publishing
A WORLD ALMANAC EDUCATION GROUP COMPANY

About the Author: Born in Mauritius, Roseline NgCheong-Lum has lived in Europe, North America, and Southeast Asia. She has traveled extensively in Europe and has a deep interest in various European cultures. She is the author of several books for children.

Written by
ROSELINE NGCHEONG-LUM

Edited by
LEELA VENGADASALAM

Designed by
LYNN CHIN

Picture research by
SUSAN JANE MANUEL

This edition first published in 2000 by
Gareth Stevens Publishing
A World Almanac Education Group Company
1555 North RiverCenter Drive, Suite 201
Milwaukee, Wisconsin 53212 USA

For a free color catalog describing
Gareth Stevens' list of high-quality books
and multimedia programs, call
1-800-542-2595 (USA) or
1-800-461-9120 (CANADA).
Gareth Stevens Publishing's
Fax: (414) 225-0377.

© **TIMES MEDIA PRIVATE LIMITED 2000**
Originated and designed by
Times Editions
An imprint of Times Media Private Limited
A member of the Times Publishing Group
Times Centre, 1 New Industrial Road
Singapore 536196
http://www.timesone.com.sg/te

Library of Congress Cataloging-in-Publication Data
NgCheong-Lum, Roseline, 1962–
Portugal / by Roseline NgCheong-Lum.
p. cm. -- (Countries of the world)
Includes bibliographical references (p. 94) and index.
Summary: An introduction to the geography, history, economy, culture, and people of Portugal.
ISBN 0-8368-2326-5 (lib. bdg.)
1. Portugal--Juvenile literature. [1. Portugal.] I. Title. II. Countries of the world (Milwaukee, Wis.)
DP517.N43   2000
946.9--dc21   99-089377

Printed in Malaysia

1 2 3 4 5 6 7 8 9 04 03 02 01 00

PICTURE CREDITS
A.N.A Press Agency: 29, 31 (bottom), 46, 67, 73 (bottom)
Giulio Andreini: 50, 51
Archive Photos: 60, 61, 75, 80
Peter Baker/International Photobank: 9 (bottom)
Jan Butchofsky: 4, 6, 11, 30, 43
Contexto Fotoarquivo: 76
Focus Team–Italy: 22, 52, 70, 71, 89
Blaine Harrington III: 10, 17, 42
HBL Network Photo Agency: 23, 27, 48, 54, 63
Dave G. Houser: 2, 3 (center), 7, 8, 9 (top), 19, 25, 26 (bottom), 31 (top), 37, 49, 53, 72
The Hutchison Library: 12, 59
Jason Laure: 5, 14, 18, 20, 21, 32, 38, 44, 56, 57, 64, 66, 68, 69 (both), 74, 78, 82 (both), 83, 84, 85, 90 (both)
North Wind Picture Archives: 13, 45 (both)
Photobank Photolibrary/Singapore: 1, 3 (top), 34, 35, 62, 87, 91
David Simson: 28, 36 (bottom), 41 (top)
Topham Picturepoint: cover, 3 (bottom), 15 (both), 16, 24, 26 (top), 33, 36 (top), 39, 40, 41 (bottom), 47, 55, 58, 65, 73 (top), 77, 79, 81

Digital Scanning by Superskill Graphics Pte Ltd

Contents

AN OVERVIEW OF PORTUGAL

Portugal is one of the oldest independent countries in the world. Its history traces periods of great wealth and expansion, and also several dark decades when the country was almost cut off from the rest of the world. This historical burden is still felt by the Portuguese people. The concept of *saudade* (sow-DAH-de), which encompasses a deep nostalgia for things past and a resigned certainty about present pains, is the defining element of the Portuguese soul. Today, Portugal is looking to join the rest of the developed world. Although still one of the poorest countries in Western Europe, Portugal has opened up its economy to foreign investments, and modernization is well underway.

Opposite: **People in traditional Portuguese costumes add to the color and fun of the many festivals that take place across Portugal every year.**

Below: **The April 25th Bridge in Lisbon, the capital of Portugal, is one of the longest suspension bridges in Europe.**

THE FLAG OF PORTUGAL

Portugal's flag dates from the 1910 revolution that overthrew the monarchy. It consists of two bands: green and red. Green symbolizes hope, while red stands for the blood shed during the revolution. In the middle is a crest over a golden armillary sphere. Inside the crest is a white shield, the armor of Afonso Henriques, the first king of Portugal (r. 1139–1185). The five blue shields represent the five Moorish kings defeated by Henriques. The dots inside the blue shields represent the five wounds of Christ. The seven castles around the white shield symbolize the fortified locations that Henriques captured from the Moors.

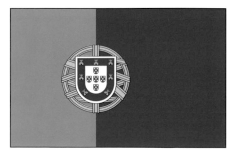

Geography

The Regions

Portugal is a thin, rectangular strip of land on the western side of the Iberian Peninsula, which includes Spain and Portugal. With an area of about 35,672 square miles (92,390 square kilometers), Portugal is no bigger than the state of Indiana. Its only neighbor is Spain. Two groups of islands in the Atlantic Ocean — the Madeira Islands and the Azores Archipelago — belong to Portugal.

Mainland Portugal has a varied landscape. Sloping from northeast to southwest, it is made up of plains broken by mountains. Northern Portugal is hilly, with huge plateaus intersected by valleys. In the northwest, the Minho and Douro Litoral regions are fertile and densely populated. Vineyards here produce most of Portugal's wines. The northeast, which consists of Trás-os-Montes, Upper Douro, and Upper Beira, is mountainous.

Alentejo, Estremadura, Lower Beira, and Beira Litoral make up the central plains. They support the cultivation of cork, wheat, tomatoes, and olive trees. The Algarve, the

Below: **Fascinating rock formations are typical of the western Algarve.**

southernmost region of Portugal, has endless beaches that attract thousands of tourists every year. Cape St. Vincent is the southwesternmost point in continental Europe. Lisbon, the capital, lies at the mouth of the Tagus (Tejo) River, which empties into the Atlantic Ocean. Lisbon is one of Portugal's few natural harbors, and most of Portugal's trade passes through the city. Another important harbor town is Oporto, or Porto, in the north, the center of the port wine trade.

Mountains and Rivers

Two natural landmarks divide the country into north and south: the Serra de Estrêla mountain range and the Tagus River. The Serra de Estrêla is the highest mountain range in Portugal. The Torre, the highest point on mainland Portugal at 6,538 feet (1,993 meters), is found here. The highest mountain in the whole of the Portuguese territory at 7,714 feet (2,351 m) is Pico Alto in the Azores.

The Tagus is the longest river in Portugal; its source lies in Spain, and it crosses the breadth of the country before flowing into the Atlantic at Lisbon. The Guadiana River in the south serves as the border between Portugal and Spain for over 30 miles (48 km).

Above: **Cabo da Roca is continental Europe's westernmost point. It lies along Portugal's western coast.**

LISBON

Ravaged by an earthquake in 1755 and later completely rebuilt, Lisbon recovered from the devastation to become one of the most beautiful, but crowded, cities in the world. It is the administrative, industrial, and economic center of Portugal and home to more than 2 million people.

(A Closer Look, page 66)

Seasons

The climate in Portugal ranges from temperate in the north to subtropical in the south. The coastal areas benefit from milder weather and less variation between the seasons. Sea breezes blowing in from the Atlantic keep summers cool and winters mild. The highest temperatures are recorded in the regions of Alentejo and Douro, where droughts can last for more than a month. August is the hottest month and January the coldest. Only the high Serra de Estrêla mountain region receives snow in the winter.

Above: **Spring brings a carpet of wildflowers to this olive grove near Évora.**

Plants and Animals

There are more than 2,500 varieties of plants in Portugal, one-third of which was brought in during Portugal's colonization period between the fifteenth and eighteenth centuries. The mountainous interior is home to European species of oak and pine, while Mediterranean trees, such as olive, almond, and cork oak, thrive in the south. Forests cover about 35 percent of the country.

Animals native to Portugal include both European and North African species. Common animals in the countryside are the small species of foxes and rabbits. Larger animals, such as deer and wild boar, are found only in the mountainous interior. The two most endangered mammals in Portugal are the Iberian wolf and the lynx. They are fully protected by the law and reside in natural parks. The Portuguese waterdog is another animal that has been rescued from the brink of extinction. Resembling a poodle, it has webbed feet that enable it to swim and dive for fish.

One of the most strictly protected reptiles is the Mediterranean chameleon. Originating in North Africa, it appeared in Portugal seventy years ago and is the only species of chameleon in Europe. Measuring about 10 inches (25.4 cm) long, it has independently moving eyes and a tongue that is longer than its body. It comes in a variety of colors.

Bird life is abundant in Portugal because the country is on the migratory route for many northern and central European species. Avocets, spoonbills, storks, and flamingos are common sights. Rare species, such as the golden eagle, the black stork, and the griffon vulture, inhabit the mountainous regions of the north. The rivers of Portugal teem with marine life, such as carp, trout, and salmon. Sardines and tuna are brought in from the Atlantic. Dolphins, however, are declining in numbers.

Above: **Chimneys are a favorite roosting spot for storks throughout the Alentejo.**

Left: **The Algarve's fertile soil supports vast plantations of almond trees and many species of plants that have colorful blossoms.**

BERLENGA ISLAND

The largest of a group of islands near Estremadura, Berlenga Island has many amazing rock formations. In the summer, the sea around the island is calm and crystal clear — a rare occurrence in the Atlantic. The rock formations, together with the varied bird life, attract many naturalists to the island every year.

(*A Closer Look, page 50*)

History

Lusitania

Portugal has been inhabited on and off since the Paleolithic period about a million years ago, when human beings first appeared on Earth. Permanent settlements in Portugal date from the second millennium B.C.

A prehistoric people known as the Iberians settled in Portugal and Spain about 5,000 years ago. In 700 B.C., Celtic invaders from central Europe made their home in the north. Of the Iberian tribes, the Lusitani were the fiercest. They gained prominence for their resistance to the Romans, who were extending the Roman empire into the Iberian Peninsula. The Lusitani were defeated after the death of their leader Viriathus in the later part of the second century B.C. In 27 B.C., central Portugal became a province of the Roman Empire called Lusitania.

The Romans established their capital at Lisbon and set out to pacify the local tribes. Their rule led to four centuries of stability and prosperity. They left a rich legacy, including the Portuguese language, which is derived from Latin; the Christian religion; an urban civilization; a network of main roads; a legal system; and the large-scale establishment of farms.

Left: **Castelo Dos Mouros was built by the Moors in the eighth or ninth century A.D. and captured by the Portuguese in 1147. The structure stands in ruins today.**

Left: Afonso Henriques was born in 1109. His father, Count Henry of Burgundy, governed northern Portugal for the Spanish king of Leon and Castile. After Henry's death, Afonso Henriques declared himself king of Portugal. Later, he consolidated his kingdom by winning back the territories to the south of the Tagus River under Moorish control. Afonso Henriques remained in power for nearly sixty years until his death in 1185.

The Moors and Independent Portugal

As the Roman Empire declined in the fifth century A.D., Lusitania was overrun by Germanic tribes, first the Suevi, and then the Visigoths. The Muslim Moors, invaders from North Africa, also had a lasting effect on the country. They defeated the Visigoths in 711 and had a strong hold on the southern part of the country. Northern Lusitania resisted Moorish rule and suffered economically. The Moors introduced new forms of irrigation, established rice fields and fruit farms in the Algarve, and developed handicrafts.

The Christian "reconquest" of the Iberian Peninsula began in the ninth century, as the small kingdoms in the north began to arm themselves against the Moors. By the eleventh century, the northern third of Portugal, called *Portucale*, was governed by one family as part of the Spanish kingdom of Leon and Castile. In 1128, Afonso Henriques declared the independence of this region from Leon and Castile and began to reclaim the rest of present-day Portugal from the Moors. The reconquest was completed in 1249 when Afonso III occupied the Algarve. Portugal has remained independent ever since.

Age of Explorations and Conquests

In the fifteenth century, Portugal entered a period of great prosperity after the exploration of lands in Africa, Asia, and America by Portuguese explorers. It all began in 1415 with the conquest of Ceuta in North Africa. Following the Christian crusading spirit of warfare against the Muslims, Portuguese kings sent more armies to Africa, capturing other Moroccan towns. This soon became a full-scale exploration, and Portuguese sailors ventured farther with each new conquest. Portugal became rich from the gold and slaves brought back from the African coast, and the discovery of a sea route to India by Vasco da Gama in 1498 made Portugal one of the greatest maritime powers of the time. Portugal controlled the Indian Ocean and the lucrative spice trade. The riches brought back from the colonies financed the building of splendid castles and monumental churches. Exploration also fostered the development of the unique Manueline style of architecture.

THE AGE OF EXPLORERS

The Portuguese were the first Europeans to sail down the coast of West Africa; discover Madeira, the Azores, and Cape Verde; round the Cape of Good Hope; reach India by sea from the west; trade with China and Japan; and settle Newfoundland. These achievements would not have been possible without the spirit of adventure of the early explorers: Bartholomeu Diaz, Vasco da Gama, and Ferdinand Magellan.
(*A Closer Look, page 44*)

Constitutional Monarchy

The period of prosperity did not last long. In 1580, Philip II of Spain claimed the Portuguese throne. Spanish rule was detrimental to Portugal, which soon lost many of its colonies to the Dutch and was heavily taxed to pay for Spain's foreign wars. Although Portuguese rule was restored in 1668 and the discovery of great amounts of gold and diamonds in Brazil boosted the Portuguese economy, the country continued to decline as a world power throughout the eighteenth century.

By the nineteenth century, Portugal was so weak that it was easily overrun by Napoleon's French army. The entire royal family fled to Brazil. Discontent was brewing in Portugal and, after Brazil declared its independence in 1822, a constitutional monarchy was proclaimed in 1826. This led to a period of chaos that culminated in a civil war in 1832 between King Pedro IV and his brother Miguel. The liberal Pedro won, and the second half of the century was much more stable, with good industrial growth.

Opposite: **The Monument of the Discoveries is on the bank of the Tagus River. It celebrates the efforts of Portuguese seamen who set out from this site in the fifteenth century on their voyages of discovery. Leading the people on the prow is Henry the Navigator.**

Below: **A seventeenth-century painting shows a busy Lisbon harbor.**

The Twentieth Century

By the twentieth century, people had begun to lose their faith in the constitutional monarchy. The Republican movement, begun in the 1890s, attacked the government for being inefficient and corrupt. When a Republican revolt failed in 1908, the Republicans murdered King Carlos I and his heir, Luis Filipe. Aided by the military, they finally overthrew the monarchy in 1910. King Manuel II, Carlos's younger son, went into exile.

In 1926, labor strikes and political instability led to a bloodless coup, in which the military took over the government. António Salazar instituted the "New State." Portugal was ruled as a police state, with strict censorship and secret police.

After World War II, the colonies began to demand their independence. Portugal had to fight costly guerilla wars in Africa. Disillusioned by the fighting in Africa, a group of military officers toppled the fascist government on April 25, 1974. Called "The Carnation Revolution," the incident got its name from the red carnations that were in season and which soldiers put in their gun barrels to protest against the wars. After a period of instability, the Portuguese opted for socialism to help them back to democracy. In 1976, the first free elections in nearly fifty years brought socialist Dr. Mário Soares to power. In 1986, Portugal was admitted into the European Union (EU).

THE FRIENDLY NEIGHBOR?

Portugal and Spain are neighbors that have not always been on good terms. Although their relationship is better now, they are still at "war" with each other; this time over water, not land.

(A Closer Look, page 62)

Below: A communist party mural points to the brief period of political instability following the Carnation Revolution. During this time, communist forces took control of the government in Lisbon. In November 1975, moderate military elements restored political order, paving the way for the adoption of a socialist constitution in 1976.

14

Henry the Navigator (1394–1460)

Prince Henry (Henrique in Portuguese) was born in Oporto in 1394. When he was eighteen, he convinced his father, King João I, to let him and his elder brothers invade Ceuta in North Africa. After his successful conquest, his fame spread throughout Europe. This was the beginning of his lifelong interest in exploration and colonization. Although nicknamed "the Navigator," Henry himself did not take part in the great voyages. His main achievement was the founding of a school of navigation in Sagres to train sailors and mapmakers. As more lands were explored by the Portuguese sailors, he turned his attention to trading in slaves and gold. Henry died of a fever at the age of sixty-six.

Henry the Navigator

Marquês de Pombal (1699–1782)

Marquês de Pombal was born in 1699. A shrewd and efficient statesman, he became prime minister of Portugal in 1756. He abolished slavery in the country, reorganized the educational system, and published a new code of laws. Pombal is best remembered for rebuilding Lisbon after the great earthquake in 1755. Upon hearing of the disaster, his first response was, "Bury the dead and feed the living." After the achievement at Lisbon, Pombal went on to build more towns in Portugal.

António de Oliveira Salazar (1889–1970)

A professor of economics, António de Oliveira Salazar was appointed finance minister when the army took over the Portuguese government in 1926. In 1932, he became the prime minister of Portugal. Salazar reorganized the economy and quickly became more powerful than the president. During his years in office, the rich became richer and the poor poorer. Human rights were curbed, censorship eliminated all anti-Salazar views, and secret police kept a watchful eye on the population. In 1968, Salazar had a stroke and became unable to rule. His regime, however, continued until the 1974 revolution. The April 25th Bridge in Lisbon was originally named Salazar Bridge upon its completion in 1966. It was renamed after the revolution.

António de Oliveira Salazar

Government and the Economy

The Republican Constitution

Portugal is a republic, with political power in the hands of an elected legislature and an elected president. The country's constitution was written on April 25, 1976, but has since been revised several times. The latest revision, approved on August 12, 1982, reduced the role of the president.

The Portuguese parliament, called the Assembly of the Republic, consists of 254 members, including four representatives

of Portuguese citizens living in other countries. Elected directly every four years, they pass the laws of the country. A system of shared representation, in which even the small parties have a chance to win seats, gives the legislature a broad range of political views. The head of state is the president, who is elected every five years. As in the United States, a Portuguese president may only serve two terms. The president appoints the prime minister and the cabinet of ministers from the majority party in the assembly. The current president, Jorge Sampaio, and prime minister, António Guterres, are both from the Socialist Party.

Above: **Guards on horses stand before the National Palace at Belem, now the residence of the president of Portugal.**

The judicial system consists of different courts. District and appeals courts hear cases at the local level. The Supreme Court sits for cases that the local courts have failed to decide. Separate courts also exist for the military and for the administrative agencies. A nine-member tribunal reviews new laws to ensure these do not conflict with the national constitution.

Provincial Administration

Mainland Portugal is divided into eighteen administrative districts, each of which elects its own governor and legislature. The towns are administered by the 305 municipal authorities, while the 4,209 parish assemblies look after villages. Assemblies are elected on a system of proportional representation.

PORTUGUESE ISLANDS

The islands of Madeira and the Azores are what remain of the once vast Portuguese empire. Macau, another Portuguese territory, was returned to Chinese rule in December 1999. Even under Portuguese administration, the population of Macau was overwhelmingly Chinese and adhered to traditional Chinese beliefs.
(A Closer Look, page 70)

In 1976 and 1980, the Madeiras and the Azores became internally autonomous areas. The Madeiras form one district, and the Azores have three districts.

Above: The Town Hall in Cascais in the Estremadura region is the summer residence of Portugal's president.

The European Union (EU)

Together with Spain, Portugal joined the EU in 1986. Although Portugal is the EU's poorest member, it has reaped many economic benefits from its participation in the union. For example, trade, investment, and tourism between Portugal and Spain have improved tremendously.

17

Trade

Portugal's main trading partners are other members of the EU, who supply half the country's food imports. Other imports include heavy equipment, machinery, and oil. Portugal exports cork, wine, textiles and footwear, and processed foods. Due to its heavy dependence on imported goods, Portugal suffers an unfavorable balance of trade.

Portugal also has trade links with its former African colonies. Angola, for example, buys more than half its imports from Portugal. Newer trading partners are the United States and Japan.

Natural Resources

The mountainous areas of Portugal contain large amounts of wolframite, a mineral. Uranium is mined in the north and copper in the south. Iron and gold are also present in small quantities. One of Portugal's biggest natural resources is water. Rivers are good sources of hydropower. The sea is another major source of revenue. Portuguese territorial waters are more than twenty times the size of the country, and fishing is a vital industry.

Below: Fishermen in Cascais bring in the catch of the day.

18

Agriculture

Agriculture employs one-third of the workforce and is the third major source of revenue for Portugal. Major crops are cork, grapes, and olives. The biggest agricultural region is the Alentejo. One feature of this region is the large farms established during Roman times. Called *latifúndios* (lah-tee-FOON-dioss), these estates used large numbers of workers who had no stake in the land they worked. After the 1974 revolution, the farms were brought under state control, but successive droughts and lack of funds and technical knowledge led to the failure of the cooperative system. Many former owners bought the land back at rock-bottom prices. The latifúndios are now making a comeback.

The Manufacturing Sector

Manufacturing has been the largest growth sector in the Portuguese economy since the country joined the EU. Starting with labor-intensive and low-cost products, such as textiles and foodstuffs, Portugal diversified into producing electrical machinery and components for export. Manufacturers in heavy industry include a car assembly plant for Volkswagen, two shipyards, oil refineries, and a steelworks.

Above: **One of Lisbon's most exciting post-modern buildings is the Amoreiras, a center for shopping and business.**

CORK AND MORE!

Portugal supplies 60 percent of the world's output of cork, twice as much as Spain. Although used mainly as stoppers for wine bottles, cork has many other functions. It is used in footwear and in decorated food boxes, a traditional craft of the Alentejo.

(A Closer Look, page 52)

People and Lifestyle

Population Makeup

The Portuguese population numbers slightly more than 10 million. It is quite homogeneous, blending the physical traits of the various peoples who have settled in the country over time. In general, the Portuguese display the Mediterranean characteristics of dark hair, brown eyes, and dark skin. They are also slightly shorter than their European neighbors. There are, however, some regional differences. Some people in the north have the fair hair and blue eyes of their Germanic ancestors, while southerners tend to be more Moorish in appearance.

A few ethnic minorities live in Portugal, mainly in Lisbon and the large cities. They include Africans from the former Portuguese colonies who settled in the country in the 1970s. With 25,000 members, the Cape Verdeans constitute the largest ethnic community in Portugal. Portugal also has a small Jewish population. In the fifteenth century, Portugal offered refuge to Jews fleeing the Spanish Inquisition. Later, however, the Jews in Portugal were also persecuted and had to flee to other parts of Europe. Today, the Jewish community numbers about 6,000.

Below: **Lisbon is a cosmopolitan city, home to people of many different nationalities.**

Rural Living

Nearly two-thirds of the Portuguese population live in rural areas, where their lifestyle is dictated by the seasons and the life cycles of crops. Mechanization, instituted since Portugal joined the EU in 1986, has driven many workers away from the fields to look for work in the larger cities.

In the mountains, village life seems to be untouched by time. In the Serra de Estrêla region, some villagers live in one-room stone houses with thatched roofs. They raise sheep for wool and milk and grow potatoes, rye, and vegetables. In those areas affected by tourism, many villagers use their traditional skills to meet the demands of the tourist market. One unique feature of life in pockets of northern Portugal is the practice of transhumance. Every year in the warmer season, sheep, cattle, goats, and even entire villages move up to higher pastures for about five months. In some parts of the country, land and animals are owned collectively by the entire village.

Fisherfolk living in coastal villages still carry on with their traditional occupation. Despite the tourists in the summer, most fishermen have not turned to more lucrative ways of earning a living. They continue going out in their little boats with trawling nets. The women sort, dry, and cook the fish.

Emigration

Portugal has one of the highest rates of emigration in Europe. It is estimated that 4 million Portuguese live overseas, especially in the United States and Brazil. While their predecessors left the country to escape the political persecution of the Salazar years, today's emigrants are motivated by economic reasons.

France has the highest concentration of "temporary" Portuguese workers in Europe, some of whom work in the country illegally. Women are usually employed as household help by well-to-do families, while men work as cleaners or café waiters. Their remittances home help boost the economy. Most emigrants come from the northern Minho, one of Portugal's poorest areas. In some villages, every household has a member working in another country. The houses receiving remittances stand out from the rest: they are large, newly built, and white, with modern household appliances. In August and during Christmas, when emigrants return to visit their families, villages come alive. Emigrants' gifts and presence lend a festive air to entire villages.

Above: **Some 35 percent of the population is concentrated in the urban areas around Lisbon and Oporto. The latter is the most densely populated part of northern Portugal.**

City Life

Life in Lisbon and the other large cities is slightly different from American urban life. Most residents live in crowded apartment blocks close to the city center. Some old buildings have not been modernized and have only the basic amenities. In Lisbon's Alfama district, for example, some streets are so narrow that they are perpetually in darkness.

Family

Family ties are strong in Portugal. Most young people live with their parents until they get married and start a family. Even then, they still maintain daily contact with their parents.

The mother is the central figure in the family. She tends to the children, prepares the family meals, and runs the entire household. Even if she holds a full-time job, she often does not get much help from her husband, although this is slowly changing.

Family gatherings are often joyous events. Baptisms, weddings, and funerals bring together everyone in the extended family. Those who have settled in other countries make it a point to return for a sibling or cousin's wedding. Funerals are usually followed by a family reunion meal, with wine and reminiscing.

TRAFFIC NIGHTMARE

Few city residents drive to work because traffic is a nightmare, and Portuguese drivers have the worst safety record in Europe. Most people take the bus or subway. Workers take a one to one-and-a-half hour lunch break, and shops also close from 1 p.m to 2.30 p.m.

Below: **A family of three enjoys an afternoon in Lisbon feeding pigeons.**

Children

In Portugal, children are considered a blessing. Other than helping out with household chores, they are not asked to do anything for the family. Young children are welcomed almost everywhere, except in the most upscale restaurants. Despite being pampered, Portuguese children are usually on their best behavior when in the presence of company.

Education

Preschool for children between the ages of three and six is free but not compulsory. Most families send their young children to preschool. Elementary school lasts nine years and is compulsory. It is provided free in state schools and for a fee at private schools. The latter are usually run by the Catholic Church. Secondary school lasts another three years.

Almost all children in the country enroll in elementary and secondary education, but many drop out to work before completing their studies. Higher education is provided by the country's eighteen universities and by regional technical colleges.

Left: **Coimbra University is very much a part of life in Coimbra, a town of fine old buildings.**

Coimbra University, founded in 1290, is one of the oldest and most respected in the world.

Above: **Graduation ceremonies at Coimbra's historic university include a lively parade through the streets of town.**

Although elementary education is free and has been compulsory since 1911, Portugal's education system is dismal. Education standards lag well behind those of other countries in the EU. Nearly one-third of the population between the ages of fifteen and sixty-four can barely read and do basic math. Fifteen percent of the total population is completely illiterate. Most of them are older people, usually women, living in remote areas.

There are a number of reasons for the poor state of the Portuguese education system. During the Salazar years, the government placed emphasis on the creation of an intellectual elite and invested very little in the education of the masses. One result of this policy is that there are still not enough schools to accommodate the entire school-going population. Children in the cities, for instance, go to school in shifts. There is also a serious shortage of teachers, partly due to the low salaries in the education sector. Since the sector is controlled by a central authority, creativity is stifled, affecting students' overall performance.

Religion

Christianity pervades almost every aspect of Portuguese life. About 95 percent of the population belongs to the Roman Catholic Church, while another 3 percent adheres to other Christian denominations.

Christianity came to Portugal in the first century A.D. and has been closely linked with the history of the country. Portugal's independence arose as part of the Christian crusade to rid Europe and Jerusalem of Muslim invaders. The spread of Christianity was one of the reasons the Portuguese embarked on their great voyages of exploration.

Today, the Catholic Church still has a powerful presence in Portuguese society. Most families attend church on Sunday, and important life events are celebrated in church. A crucifix or saint's picture usually hangs above the doorway of houses, cafés, and barber shops. Saints' days and other religious festivals are celebrated with great passion. Every town or village has its own patron saint, and, in remote villages, the local church is the center of activity. Specific saints are worshiped for various reasons; for example, Saint Anthony, one of Portugal's most beloved saints, is called upon to help locate lost items.

THE CULT OF FÁTIMA

Every year on May 13 and October 13, thousands of pilgrims gather at a huge sanctuary in Fátima to worship the Virgin Mary. The church's stained glass windows tell the story of the apparitions that started the pilgrimages.
(*A Closer Look, page 54*)

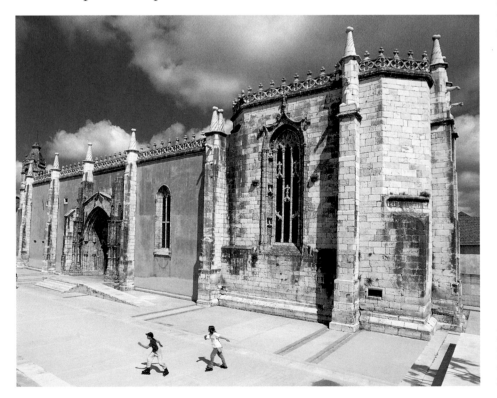

Left: Christianity is the main religion of Portugal. This fifteenth-century Church of Jesus is found in Setúbal.

Pilgrimages are an important aspect of the Roman Catholic faith. The most popular center for pilgrims is the shrine of Fátima. Twice a year, in May and October, hundreds of thousands of pilgrims come from all over the world to express their devotion to the Virgin Mary. Another important pilgrimage center is the Church of Bom Jesus in Braga. Pilgrims climb a giant zigzagging staircase on their knees to reach the church, which is on a hilltop.

Above: **Portuguese Muslims are free to practice their religion.**

People of Other Faiths

In addition to other Christian denominations, such as Anglicans, Baptists, and Methodists, Portugal's population includes about 15,000 Muslims and 6,000 Jews. They are all guaranteed freedom to worship. The Muslim community is mostly congregated in the southern part of the country, where Moorish influence is strongest. The Jews live mainly in Lisbon and Belmonte. Many Jews were forced to convert to Christianity in the sixteenth century, and, today, a good number of Portuguese trace their ancestry back to these converts. Some of them, mainly in Belmonte and Oporto, have returned to Judaism.

ALCOBAÇA

The Monastery of Alcobaça is one of the most magnificent and opulent buildings in Portugal. Despite its dissolution in 1834, Alcobaça is one of Europe's most significant medieval Cistercian monuments.

(A Closer Look, page 46)

Language and Literature

The Portuguese Language

The language of Portugal is derived from the Latin spoken by the early Roman settlers. Portuguese is similar to other Romance languages, such as French, Spanish, and Romanian. Written Portuguese is quite close to French and Spanish. The spoken language, however, sounds more like Romanian.

Portuguese pronunciation is quite difficult. Accents give different intonations to vowels and consonants. Many consonants are also slurred, making the language sound "slushy." The letter "s" is pronounced "sh" when it comes before a consonant or at the end of a word. Cascais, a town popular with tourists, actually sounds like "kashkaish." The letter "j" is always pronounced like the "s" in "treasure." Vowels on their own are quite easily pronounced, but two or three vowels together, plus an accent, renders the pronunciation trickier. The word "não," for example, sounds like the English "now."

Opposite: **Fernando Pessoa (1888–1935) was a leading contemporary poet and critic. A statue of him can be found in front of his favorite café, "A Brasileira," in Lisbon. A prolific writer, Pessoa wrote in various styles, using a different pen name for each style.**

Left: **Signs written in both Portuguese and English are placed in some areas of Portugal, especially those places frequented by tourists.**

THE LUSOPHONE MOVEMENT

The Lusophone movement, or the Comunidade dos Países de Língua Portuguesa (CPLP), unites people from all over the world who share a common language and culture. In former Portuguese colonies, the CPLP has been successful in the development and study of Portuguese language and literature.
(A Closer Look, page 68)

Portuguese Literature

Portugal has a long literary tradition, with many songs and poems dating from the twelfth century. Two of the country's kings, Afonso III and Dinis, were accomplished poets. Prose writing started at the end of the Middle Ages when philosophical books, historical and religious treatises, and chronicles of the kings' lives flourished. Theater appeared in the fifteenth century when Gil Vicente used his plays to parody contemporary beliefs and customs. The most important work in Portuguese literature is *The Lusiads*. Written in 1572 by one of the greatest European writers, Luís Vaz de Camões, the epic poem is a dramatized account of Vasco da Gama's voyage to India. The poem also recounts the history of Portugal.

In the twentieth century, writers have concentrated on rural life and nationalistic themes. During the censorship years of the Salazar regime, many political works were written but remained unpublished until the 1970s. The second half of the twentieth century saw the rise of African writers from former Portuguese colonies, such as Angolan Luandino Vieira, expressing themselves in Portuguese.

FAST FACTS

Portuguese is the fifth most widely spoken language in the world. More than 180 million people speak it in Portugal and Brazil. The language, or dialects derived from it, is also spoken in Asian regions such as Macau, East Timor, Malacca in Malaysia, and Goa in India. When Jose Saramago was awarded the Nobel Prize for Literature in 1998, the whole Lusophone (Portuguese-speaking) world celebrated. It was considered an honor for the Portuguese language itself as well as for the writer.

Arts

Painting

Portugal's oldest paintings date from the Paleolithic Age. The rock art of Foz Côa is about 25,000 years old and one of the earliest examples of art in Europe. Later artists were heavily influenced by French, Flemish, and Spanish styles. The strengths of Portuguese artists throughout the ages have been realism and portraiture. They were much less successful with imaginative themes, such as mythology and history.

The first truly Portuguese painter was Nuno Gonçalves, who lived in the fifteenth century. He and his fellow painters of the "Portuguese school" painted only religious subjects, with special emphasis on portraiture. Gonçalves's masterpiece is the *Saint Vincent Altarpiece* (1467–1470), a realistic set of panels depicting the saint receiving homage from all ranks of society. Other artists who excelled in portraits were Grão Vasco and Gaspar Vaz. These two painters of the Age of Discoveries used bright colors to paint realistic and delicate portraits.

FOZ CÔA: ART IN STONE

Plans to build a dam near the mouth of the Côa River sparked protests, which succeeded in putting a stop to the construction. The reason — the rare paintings of Foz Côa. If plans for the dam had gone ahead, the site would have been submerged, and the 25,000-year-old drawings forever lost.
(*A Closer Look, page 60*)

Below: **Old sculptures around Lisbon receive repairs.**

Left: **The Mosteiro dos Jerónimos de Belém in Belem is an excellent example of Manueline architecture. Many people believe this monastery is the crowning glory of Belem.**

One of the few female artists to gain lasting recognition was Josefa de Óbidos. Born in 1634 and taught by her father, she specialized in still lifes and detailed religious works. Another outstanding female artist was Maria Helena Vieria da Silva (1908–1992), Portugal's finest abstract painter.

Amadeo de Souza Cardoso (1887–1918) is probably the best-known Portuguese artist of the twentieth century. A student of French impressionist painter Cézanne, he invented his own style of Portuguese impressionism.

Architecture

One interesting feature of Portuguese architecture is the low, rectangular designs. Romanesque and Renaissance styles, based on the solidity of Roman construction, were favored over Gothic or Baroque. Built from granite, churches and palaces are shaped like crosses, with smooth columns and semicircular arches.

It is in surface ornamentation that Portuguese builders have given free rein to their imaginations. The Manueline style, for instance, displays an open aversion to plain surfaces. Every square inch of wall, door, or window is decorated with stone or wood sculpture. One uniquely Portuguese phenomenon is covering the entire church interior with carved and gilded wood, such as in the Convent of Jesus in Aveiro. Other interesting features are pictorial compositions made of *azulejos* (ah-zoo-LAY-shoss), or colorful tiles.

AZULEJOS

Azulejos are colorful tiles that adorn buildings and houses. Often, whole house fronts are covered with such tiles. The town of Ovar in Beira Litoral is strikingly beautiful because many house facades are decorated with bright yellow and blue azulejos.
(A Closer Look, page 48)

Music

Portuguese folk music has hardly changed since the Middle Ages. Songs often use various agricultural occupations as topics and can best be described as a kind of repetitive wailing. Bagpipes, harmonicas, accordions, flutes, drums, and countless percussion instruments add to the charm of the music. The country is famous for its strings, which include violins, the classic twelve-stringed Portuguese guitar, and six varieties of "viola-guitars." Each of these has a character, tuning, and design of its own. Best known are the four-stringed *cavaquinho* (ka-va-KEEN-noh) and the bigger *guitarra portuguesa* (gi-TAR-rah por-tu-GEH-sah), standard accompaniments to *fado* (FAH-doh).

Fado

Fado is often described as a kind of working-class blues. Derived from medieval troubadours' songs and influenced by African slave rhythms, these melancholic chants originated in eighteenth-century Lisbon. They are sung by a performer who is accompanied by one or two guitarists playing the twelve-string Portuguese guitar. Written in four-line stanzas, fado is about fate. These songs deal with the certainties of life and the sufferings and happiness that are a part of life for everyone. The Portuguese soul truly comes through in fado. Usually sad in tone, the music expresses poignantly the notion of saudade.

Opposite: Dressed in bright costumes, folk dancers in the countryside move enthusiastically to the beat of a popular tune.

Left: The Fado Museum in Lisbon is a tribute to Lisbon's unique music history.

EXPO '98

More than 15 million people from all over the world visited Expo '98, the last World Exposition of the twentieth century. Expo '98 featured five main pavilions: the Ocean Pavilion, Sea Pavilion, Pavilion of the Future, Utopia Pavilion, and the Portuguese National Pavilion.

(*A Closer Look, page 56*)

TRADITIONAL CRAFTS

Among Portuguese handicrafts, ceramics are one of the most impressive. Aside from utilitarian items, such as kitchen utensils and crockery, Portuguese potters produce an array of brightly colored figurines. The Portuguese are also known for their lace making and embroidery skills, and Madeira is one of the best centers for this craft. Long famous for its lace, Vila do Conde is one of the few places in the country with an active school for lace making. Founded in 1918, the school offers instruction to children as young as four or five. It also has a lace display that took over two years to make and used 1,400 bobbins of thread.

There are essentially two types of fado: the Lisbon fado and the fado from the university town of Coimbra. The Lisbon fado is usually performed in nightclubs and is considered more genuine. The Coimbra style is sung by men only because the songs are about feminine beauty.

Dancing

The dance scene in Portugal is vibrant, with stylistic contributions from the various regions and former colonies. The Gulbenkian Foundation has a ballet company that performs classical and contemporary ballet in Lisbon. The troupe also performs at the Algarve Music Festival in the summer.

Traditional folk dancing is alive and well in Portugal. Each region has its own variations, and folk dancers emerge in full force during festivals. During the annual National Folklore Festival in the Algarve, music and dance groups from across the country converge on various southern towns to share their regional traditions. The dances of the north have been most resistant to change. One of the most interesting is the stick dance performed by the men of Trás-os-Montes. Dressed in white shirts and skirts, and black vests and aprons, and accompanied by drums and bagpipes, the dancers put on a spectacular performance.

GULBENKIAN'S LEGACY

The Calouste Gulbenkian Museum in Lisbon and the Gulbenkian Foundation, a trust fund, were set up in honor of Calouste Sarkis Gulbenkian, an Armenian art collector who made Portugal his home until his death in 1955. The foundation promotes cultural activities.

(A Closer Look, page 64)

Leisure and Festivals

Leisure Activities

The Portuguese people treasure their leisure time, and weekends are reserved for outings to the park or museum, sports practice, and family activities. A habit that Portuguese men share with other Mediterranean males is visiting local cafés. On weekends and in the evenings, men in towns and villages gather over coffee or wine in the cafés and squares to gossip and watch the world go by. Women prefer to meet for afternoon tea sessions. Portuguese women meet their friends in a tea room or cake shop to talk about their children and swap news.

Children's Pastimes

Portuguese children have more than enough time for leisure activities since school lasts only half a day, and the amount of homework is manageable. On weekends and after school, many youngsters take part in sports practice, mainly soccer for the boys and any ball game for the girls. Many of them are also members of youth groups, such as the Scouts and Guides. On their own at home, many children like to watch television, read, or pursue hobbies.

Below: **In summer, the cool waters of Estoril beach are a welcome relief for Portuguese and tourists alike.**

Left: Spectators
expect bullfighters to
display courage, good
horsemanship, and
elegance in a fight.

Bullfighting

Bullfighting is a popular spectator sport in Portugal, although
animal rights are increasingly recognized in the country. Unlike
Spanish bullfights, the bull is not killed at the end of a fight;
rather, it is led out of the ring. The aim of the bullfight is for the
cavaleiro (ka-val-EY-roh), or bullfighter on a horse, to lodge a
series of short darts in the bull's shoulders, symbolizing the kill.
Besides courage, the cavaleiro has to display great horsemanship.
He usually demonstrates a few dressage techniques to entertain
the spectators. His performance is judged on style and courage.

A bullfight begins with the cavaleiro riding into the ring
dressed in a traditional costume complete with a tricorn hat. A
group of footmen wave their red capes to distract the bull, while
the cavaleiro sizes up the animal. He then gallops to within inches
of the bull and plants a number of darts into the animal's neck.
The last phase of the fight consists of eight young men walking
up to the bull in a single line. As the leader grabs the bull's horns,
which are sheathed to protect the bullfighter, the others pile up
behind him to lend support, and one of them takes hold of the
tail. The match ends when the bull is brought to a standstill.

Soccer Craze

Portugal is truly a soccer-crazy country. Almost every town or village boasts its own soccer team, and matches between the big teams attract thousands of spectators. Thousands more crowd into bars and cafés to watch matches shown on television.

The Best Teams

The top three soccer teams are Benfica and Sporting from Lisbon, and FC Porto. Most Portuguese soccer fans support one of these three teams. Benfica was one of Europe's finest teams in the 1960s, while FC Porto reigned supreme in 1987 when it won the European Cup, the World Club Cup, and the European Super Cup.

Eusebio

The Portuguese national soccer team had its days of glory in the 1960s when it reached the quarterfinals of the 1966 World Cup competition. Eusebio, who was a member of that team, is Portugal's most venerated player. Born in Mozambique, he was a brilliant scorer and playmaker.

Above: Eusebio, who played with Benfica, represented Portugal in international matches, scoring many goals.

Below: A boy hones his dribbling skills playing soccer on a beach.

Other Sports

Portuguese athletes excel in track and field events, especially long distance running. Marathoners Carlos Lopes, Rosa Mota, and Manuela Machado won gold medals at the Olympic Games in 1984, 1988, and 1996 respectively. Portugal hosts its own international marathon. Called the Discoveries Marathon, it is held in Lisbon every November, and top athletes fly in from all over the world to take part.

The Portuguese obsession with speed is satisfied at the annual Formula One Grand Prix of Portugal held in September at the Estoril Autodrome. Car racing is so popular that a Grand Prix is also held in the streets of Macau for Formula Three cars, which have smaller engines than Formula One cars.

Golf is another popular sport with locals as well as tourists. With eleven world-class championship courses, Portugal organizes a Golf Open every year in March.

Above: **A cycling competition is in full swing in the Alentejo, with bystanders cheering on the cyclists.**

National Days

The Portuguese celebrate their nationalism on four occasions each year. Portugal Day on June 10 is the main holiday. Another name for this day is Camões and the Communities Day, in commemoration of the country's finest poet and patriot. Independence Day on December 1 celebrates the restoration of the country's sovereignty from Spain in 1640, while Republic Day commemorates the overthrow of the monarchy and declaration of the republic on October 5, 1910. The most recently dedicated holiday is Liberty Day on April 25. It celebrates the revolution that brought back freedom and democracy to Portugal in 1974.

Christmas

Christmas is an important day for children. Instead of writing to Santa Claus, they ask Baby Jesus in the nativity crib for presents. Everyone goes to midnight mass and eats a supper of *bacalhau* (bah-kahl-O), or dried codfish. The main dish on Christmas Day is roast turkey followed by *bolo rei* (boh-lo RAY), a type of doughnut coated in glazed fruit, crushed nuts, and sugar icing. Inside is a dry bean. Whoever gets the bean has to pay for the cake or buy another one on December 31.

Below: **The Portuguese celebrate Liberty Day by marching through the streets bearing red carnations, in memory of the soldiers who put carnations, as symbols of peace, into the barrels of their guns on April 25, 1974.**

Left: Romaria participants in Minho get dressed up in colorful costumes to celebrate.

Holy Week

For the Portuguese, Holy Week is the most spectacular holiday in the Christian calendar, especially in Braga. Many processions are held during the week, the most amazing of which is Braga's Senhor Ecce Homo on Maundy Thursday. Bearing torches, black-hooded penitents walk through the streets toward the cathedral. On Good Friday, an effigy of a bleeding Christ is carried through some villages. Easter Sunday starts with a church service, after which the parish priest walks along the streets with a crucifix on a tall staff so parishioners can kiss the feet of Jesus.

Romaria

A *romaria* (roh-mah-ree-AH) is a religious festival honoring a saint and usually takes the form of a pilgrimage to a shrine or church. Although the devotees come to pray and ask for favors, there is still much merrymaking with music, food, and folk dancing. Because the Portuguese are devout Catholics, a romaria takes place almost every day of the year in different parts of Portugal. Those in the north are the most traditional and spectacular.

THE FESTIVAL OF TRAYS

The Festival of Trays is a five-day-long festival celebrated in central Portugal. It ends with a unique procession in which young girls balance trays of bread on their heads with help from their escorts. Fireworks, music, and dancing make the Festival of Trays truly memorable.
(A Closer Look, page 58)

Food

Regional Specialties

Portuguese regional cuisine varies with the ingredients that are available in the area. Fish and shellfish dishes are common along the coast. One of the most unusual dishes is fish soup from the Lisbon coast. Shellfish are added to a thick soup of mashed bread, oil, garlic, and coriander. Another interesting dish is the seafood *cataplana* (ka-ta-PLAN-na) from the Algarve. Fish and shellfish are cooked in a copper pan shaped like a clam.

In the north, pork meat and pork products are very popular. Besides the usual hams and sausages, northerners also like to eat blood sausage. Oporto is famous for its tripe stew. According to folklore, the people of Oporto sent their best meat to Prince Henry the Navigator when he was preparing to sail for Morocco, and kept only the offal, or innards, for themselves. Since then, northerners have developed a taste for pig intestines.

Left: The Portuguese will travel for miles just to eat the specialty of a region, such as crabs and lobsters along the coast.

Traditional Favorites

The most beloved dish in Portugal is bacalhau. The Portuguese say that there are more ways of cooking this dried codfish than there are days in a year. The Portuguese love affair with codfish began in the sixteenth century when sailors first started to fish off the coast of Newfoundland. Bacalhau is so popular that it is known as "the faithful friend." Today, the fish is imported from Norway. Although expensive, it more than doubles in volume after soaking, keeps well, and is extremely nourishing. Bacalhau is stewed with potatoes, deep-fried, scrambled with eggs, and cooked in many other ways.

Originating in the northern Minho region, *caldo verde* (KAL-do VEHR-duh) is now a popular dish across Portugal. The soup takes its green color from the shredded green cabbage that is added at the last stage of cooking. Its other ingredients are smoked sausage, onions, potatoes, and garlic. Eaten with thick slices of bread, caldo verde is a satisfying and nutritious meal.

The Portuguese have a sweet tooth and have created a huge variety of desserts and pastries. Most of them are made with egg, almond, and sugar. Traditional favorites are baked custard and rice pudding. Many of these recipes date back to the eighteenth century.

WINES OF PORTUGAL

Portugal's three main types of wines are *vinho verde* (VEE-nyo VEHR-duh), Madeira, and port. The last is the most popular. A sweet wine, port is made from grapes and fortified by the addition of grape brandy before being matured in oak casks.

(A Closer Look, page 72)

A CLOSER LOOK AT PORTUGAL

The great explorers of the fifteenth and sixteenth centuries not only brought riches to Portugal but also opened up new worlds and possibilities for humankind. One legacy of this empire-building period is the Lusophone movement, which brings together people from various continents who share the Portuguese language and culture. The most important benefactor of the Portuguese people in the twentieth century, however, had no Lusophone ties. Calouste Sarkis Gulbenkian was an Armenian who bequeathed his fortune to the country and began the Gulbenkian Foundation, a trust fund for cultural advancement.

Opposite: An *elevador* (ee-li-va-DOR), or cable car, allows people in Lisbon to travel easily within the city.

Above: A fisherman in Setúbal does some repairs on his wooden fishing boat.

Culture and the arts have always been important to the Portuguese people. Lisbon, the capital, was voted the European City of Culture in 1994. The Manueline style is a distinctive style of Portuguese architecture, of which the Monastery of Alcobaça is a splendid example. This monument is on the World Heritage list of UNESCO (United Nations Educational, Scientific, and Cultural Organization). Another important site is Foz Côa, which contains the largest collection of prehistoric rock drawings in Europe. The Portuguese people also express themselves beautifully in their songs. The fado, for instance, gives voice to the Portuguese soul.

The Age of Explorers

The golden age of Portuguese exploration took place between 1419 and 1500. Under the patronage of Prince Henry the Navigator and with the help of newly designed caravels, Portuguese seafarers set out to "discover" the rest of the world (the lands beyond Europe), turning Portugal into one of the richest nations in the world. Buoyed by the conquest of Ceuta in North Africa in 1415, Prince Henry set up a School of Navigation in Sagres and trained many sailors to brave the unknown seas.

Left: **Portuguese explorers sailed in caravels to discover new lands.**

Bartholomeu Diaz (1450–1500)

Born in 1450, Bartholomeu Diaz was the first navigator to round the Cape of Good Hope at the southern tip of Africa. In 1481, he commanded a vessel in a fleet that sailed down the Gold Coast of Africa. Five years later, the Portuguese king sent him to explore the rest of the western coast of Africa. He set sail from Lisbon in August 1487 and, six months later, he rounded the southern end of the African continent, opening a way for explorers to find a route to the Far East. On his return voyage, he named the Cape of Good Hope. Diaz died in 1500 on the expedition with Pedro Álvares Cabral that led to the exploration of Brazil.

Vasco da Gama (1460–1524)

The son of a well-known sailor, Vasco da Gama was born in 1460. In 1497, King Manuel I sent him on a voyage to find a sea route to India by sailing around Africa. After fighting Arab traders in Mozambique and finding a guide in Kenya, his ships arrived in India in 1498. Despite the hostile locals, he left a few men and traded with the Indians. When da Gama went home to Portugal, he received a hero's welcome and was named Admiral of the Sea of India. Four years later, he returned to India and died there in 1524 as the Viceroy of India.

Vasco da Gama

Ferdinand Magellan (1480–1521)

Born in 1480, Ferdinand Magellan was fascinated by the voyages of Christopher Columbus and Vasco da Gama. His first trip was in 1505 when he went to India with Portugal's first viceroy to that country. In September 1519, Magellan set sail from Spain to find a westward route to the Spice Islands in the East Indies. It was more than a year later, in October 1520, that he found a passage to the Pacific Ocean at the tip of South America, now known as the Strait of Magellan. When he saw the ocean, he named it "Pacific" because it seemed so peaceful compared to the stormy Atlantic. The discovery of the Magellan Strait made possible the exploration of the Pacific. Magellan and his crew were the first Europeans to sail across the Pacific. They found the Spice Islands in 1521, and his crew eventually sailed back to Europe. In 1521, Magellan was killed in a battle with Philippine natives. This voyage proved for the first time that the world was round.

Ferdinand Magellan

Alcobaça

One of the most impressive Gothic monuments in Portugal is the Monastery of Alcobaça in the province of Estremadura. Founded in 1153 by Afonso Henriques to celebrate his 1147 victory over the Moors, the monastery formed the most powerful religious order in the country by the end of the thirteenth century — the Cistercian order.

Alcobaça stands in a fertile area, and the Cistercian monks were agricultural experts. The monastery owned vast tracts of farmland, orchards, and vineyards, and soon acquired a fine reputation for hospitality, generosity, and charity. Because of its agricultural heritage, the surrounding area is still one of the most productive regions in Portugal. In the thirteenth century, the monks switched from farming to teaching. With money from renting the estate to peasant farmers, the monks built one of the largest libraries in the country. The seventeenth century saw another switch, this time to pottery and sculpture. The residents of Alcobaça turned out beautiful figures in stone, wood, and clay. By the time the monastery was dissolved in 1834, the monks had gone back to their original vocation — farming.

Left: **The Monastery of Alcobaça is one of the largest monasteries in Portugal.**

Left: **In the cloister of the Alcobaça Abbey is a well house.**

A Stream Runs Through It

In its heyday, the Monastery of Alcobaça was so rich that the monks' extravagance became legendary. One eighteenth-century English traveler recounted how the monks indulged in daily banquets and drank more wine than he had ever seen. The kitchen was the focal point of the monastery. This room had a big chimney and cellars full of wine. A stream from a nearby river ran through the room. It was used for washing and cooking, and also as a constant source of fresh fish, which plopped out into a stone basin. A large number of cooks and attendants were employed to turn out gargantuan meals every day. Overindulgence, however, was not condoned and, as a practical test for obesity, the monks had to file through a narrow door on their way to the refectory (dining hall). Those who could not make it past the doorway were forced to fast until they could squeeze in!

Now on UNESCO's World Heritage list, the Monastery of Alcobaça is the burial place of Pedro and Inês de Castro, romantic figures in Portuguese history. Under the orders of Pedro, their tombs are placed foot to foot so that when they rise on Judgment Day, they will see each other first.

FORBIDDEN LOVE

Inês de Castro was the daughter of a Spanish nobleman. When Pedro, heir to the Portuguese throne, fell in love with her, King Afonso IV forbade their marriage. The two lovers disobeyed the king's orders and were married secretly. At the news of their marriage, Afonso IV ordered Inês's death. When Pedro became king in 1357, he took revenge by killing Inês's murderers. As a sign of his love for Inês, he removed her body from its tomb, crowned the corpse, and made the entire royal circle acknowledge her as queen by kissing her decomposing hand.

Azulejos

Art on Tiles

Colorful tiles began to brighten up Portuguese and Spanish buildings during the Middle Ages when the Moors conquered most of the Iberian Peninsula. Called azulejos, these tiles derive their name from the Arabic word *al zuleiq*, meaning small, polished stone. Portuguese azulejos are the most artistic in the world, and many murals are bright, beautiful works of art. The blue and white tiles of the Baroque period are considered the finest of all tiles.

After the Moors were expelled from Spain at the end of the sixteenth century, and Moorish-made tiles were no longer available, many azulejo factories were established in Portugal, mainly in Lisbon, Oporto, and Coimbra. Unlike Moorish tiles, Portuguese azulejos are not made in relief patterns, but are flat like Italian and Flemish majolica. The tiles are given a white tin glaze, and the designs are painted in metallic pigments.

Below: **Tile-clad houses have many advantages over stone or plaster surfaces. In addition to their pretty designs, tiles are relatively cheap and easy to maintain. They retain a fresh appearance with just a wash from time to time. They also give the building a trim and neat look.**

Tiles with History

One of the most important tile artworks is the blue and white wall mural depicting a panoramic view of Lisbon before the 1755 earthquake. It is one of the few images of Lisbon before the quake. Production of azulejos flourished after the quake because the reconstruction of the town required a large number of tiles. In order to produce them faster, simpler designs were created.

In the seventeenth century, tile "tapestries" became very popular. These had a great variety of designs in blue, white, and yellow. Mass production began in 1767 when King José established the Royal Factory at Lisbon, but only churches, fountains, and palaces were adorned with these highly decorative tiles. When the court fled to Brazil in the early nineteenth century, production of azulejos ceased almost completely. Azulejos enjoyed a revival in the middle of the century when middle-class households, public buildings, and commercial premises used them for both indoor and outdoor decoration.

Today, the three main azulejo factories in Lisbon concentrate on reproductions of old designs and export most of their output to the United States, the Netherlands, and Germany.

Above: **Azulejos and ceramic handicrafts are specialties of Portugal.**

Berlenga Island

Rocks of Beauty

On the Atlantic coast, just north of Lisbon, lies a rather startling island. Berlenga Island is the largest of a group of islands about 7 miles (11.3 km) from Peniche, a traditional fishing village. Only 1 square mile (2.59 sq km) in area, Berlenga gives the impression of a Scottish island transported south. Instead of the more usual sand and gravel beaches found in this region, the coastline is jagged and filled with grottoes. Miniature fjords abound, and the entire place displays extraordinary rock formations.

Berlenga was once inhabited by monks who spent their time praying and rescuing sailors in distress. They were so troubled by pirates that they had to rebuild their monastery as a fort on a nearby islet to the southeast. The seventeenth-century stone Fort of Saint John the Baptist is joined to Berlenga Island by a short and narrow causeway. For centuries, this five-sided stark building suffered repeated assaults from pirates and foreign armies. It is now a hostel for tourists.

Below: **Most people in Peniche depend on fishing for a living.**

Above: **Grottoes and rock formations characterize Berlenga Island's coastline.**

Since the island is a nature reserve, only a couple dozen fishermen are allowed to live there. It can, however, get quite crowded and noisy during the summer when tourists come to visit the old monastery and see the wildlife. It takes about an hour to get to the island by ferry from the mainland. The center of activity is the main landing dock where the fishermen moor their colorful boats. The only buildings on Berlenga are a cluster of huts for the fishermen, a basic shop, a bar-cum-restaurant, and a lighthouse. One interesting geographical feature is the Furado Grande, a fantastic marine tunnel measuring 230 feet (70 m). It culminates in the precipitous red granite cliffs of Dream Cove. Only the adventurous sail through the tunnel in their small boats.

Berlenga is home to thousands of sea birds, including herring gulls, guillemots, puffins, and cormorants. They can be found in every nook and cranny of the island. Visitors are only allowed on makeshift paths marked with stones. Those who stray from the designated paths are guided back by rangers stationed on the island. The main "danger" of visiting a place with so much bird life is the risk of getting hit with bird droppings. Most tourists keep their eyes peeled as much to admire the birds as to avoid becoming the target of some mischievous gull.

Cork and More!

Not Just a Bottle Stopper

Cork is an essential ingredient in the wine industry. Cork that seals a wine bottle is more than just a stopper to prevent liquid from flowing out of the bottle. It helps the wine develop its own distinct flavor. Being tasteless, odorless, and non-toxic, cork does not interfere with the wine-aging process, making it the perfect seal for wines and champagnes. Portugal is the largest producer of cork in the world, turning out about 30 million corks a day. There are about 700 factories in Portugal, and one family-run

firm, Corticeira Amorim, accounts for one-third of the total national production of cork.

Above: **Wine matures gently and keeps longer in airtight glass bottles with cork stoppers.**

In the seventeenth century, Dom Perignon, the wine-making monk, popularized the use of cork as a stopper for champagne bottles. Champagne makers are particularly fussy about the cork they use. Only the best cork will capture the fine bubbles associated with the spirit, resulting in the distinct popping sound the bottle makes upon being opened. The champagne industry alone uses 500 million corks a year.

Cork is made from the bark of the cork oak, which grows well throughout Portugal. Cork oak is a tall, round-topped evergreen with glossy, holly-like leaves and wrinkled bark. Cork oak takes about twenty years to mature, and a law prevents growers from cutting its bark before it reaches a certain circumference (usually when it is about fifteen years old). A tree needs to be about thirty years old for its bark to have commercial value.

Farmers strip the bark of cork oaks in summer and roll it up to take to the processing factory. Cork cutting is done by hand, and cutters have to be careful not to damage the inner layers of the trunk. The tree is then left with a naked reddish-colored trunk until it grows new bark. This process takes about ten years before the tree is stripped again. A cork oak has a lifespan of about one hundred years, yielding about eight

harvests in its lifetime. The best quality cork comes from mature trees. The center of the cork industry is the Alentejo, where about 2,700 square miles (6,993 square km) of land are under cultivation. Cork oak provides welcome shade and revenue in this arid region.

Cork is a prized material not only in the manufacture of bottle stoppers. Its insulating and watertight qualities also make it perfect for a variety of products, from footwear, gaskets, and girders to baseball bats. In the rural areas, cork helps produce waterproof and heat-proof food containers. One of the traditional crafts of the Alentejo is decorated food boxes made of cork.

Above: **To date, no substitute for cork has been found. Cork oak is therefore very valuable.**

The Cult of Fátima

Secrets Revealed: All but One

One of the greatest centers of Roman Catholic devotion is the shrine of Fátima in central Portugal. The cult of Fátima evolved from a vision seen by three shepherd children during World War I. On May 13, 1917, ten-year-old Lucia Santos and her cousins, Francisco and Jacinta Marta, saw a shining figure, believed to be the Virgin Mary, in an oak tree. The apparition told the children to come back every month on the same day for six months.

In July 1917, the Virgin Mary told Lucia the three "Secrets of Fátima." The first secret was a message of peace: World War I would end soon, and people would live in peace. The second foresaw the onset of atheism in Russia and the start of World War II. The third secret has never been divulged because it apparently refers to a disaster so terrible "the living would envy the dead." This secret was written down by Lucia in 1944 and has been kept by the Vatican since 1957. Only the Pope can read it. Francisco and Jacinta Marta died in their youth, and they are buried in the Fátima Basilica. Lucia became a Carmelite nun and is still alive.

Below: **Most pilgrims approach the shrine of the Virgin Mary in prayer on bended knees. Some bring flowers to leave at the shrine.**

Every year, on May 13 and October 13, the dates of the first and last apparitions, thousands of pilgrims arrive in Fátima to worship the Virgin Mary. They converge on the basilica that was built in 1928 to commemorate the phenomenon. The precinct is built on an enormous scale to accommodate all the pilgrims. Its esplanade, an open, level space, is twice the size of St. Peter's Square in Rome. On the esplanade stands a small chapel marking the exact spot where the apparitions appeared. Inside the chapel is a statue of the Virgin Mary. Its crown holds the bullet extracted from Pope John Paul II after an assassination attempt on him in 1981.

The most impressive sight, however, is not the grandeur of the buildings but the expressions of emotion and faith on the pilgrims' faces. Most of them approach the shrine on their knees as a sign of penitence. Those who have been cured of diseases through their devotion bring wax limbs to burn as offerings. The pilgrims believe deeply that miracles can occur, and many come to seek help to restore their health. Services are held at night and are attended by thousands of people holding lighted candles.

Expo '98

In 1998, Portugal played host to the last World Exposition of the twentieth century. Since 1998 was decreed Year of the Ocean by the United Nations, the theme of the fair was "The Ocean, the Heritage for the Future." This tied in well with Portugal's history of maritime exploration and also with the 500th anniversary celebration of Vasco da Gama's first sea voyage to India.

The Portuguese spared no effort in making their capital fit for visitors. Lisbon underwent its biggest facelift since the 1755 earthquake. A 3-mile-long (4.8-km-long) stretch of Lisbon's waterfront was renovated to accommodate the hundreds of pavilions built on the aquatic theme. A new 8-mile (12.9-km) bridge was built across the Tagus River, a railway station was established, and an underground link connected the city to the exposition site.

Pavilions of Water

The exhibition, centered around five main pavilions, gave the site the appearance of a theme park. The most impressive was the Ocean Pavilion, which hovered spectacularly over the Tagus

Below: **The Utopia Pavilion was one of the five major pavilions at Expo '98, which started on May 22 and ended on September 30.**

River. Housing the largest aquarium in Europe, it reconstructed the ecosystems of the North Atlantic, Indian, Antarctic, and Pacific oceans. With more than 25,000 fish, birds, and mammals, the Ocean Pavilion was the center of attraction at Expo '98. At the Knowledge of the Sea Pavilion, visitors learned how to protect the sea. The Pavilion of the Future made people aware of the future of oceans by examining current problems and exploring ways in which to control damage already done to oceans. The Utopia Pavilion featured an unusual audiovisual journey, from deep under the sea to the limits of the universe. Finally, the Portuguese National Pavilion showcased the discoveries of the Portuguese people and the spirit of adventure of the human race.

More than 150 countries set up pavilions at the fair. The British Pavilion featured a spiral moving walkway, which took visitors through a simulated seascape. Germany's pavilion offered a virtual reality dive down to a submerged station more than 300 feet (91 m) underwater.

Above: **A band from the United States lends a festive air to Expo '98. One of the most popular sites at the fair was the U.S. Pavilion. It celebrated America's commitment to exploring and preserving the oceans. More than 9,000 people walked through it every day, trying out hands-on displays.**

The Festival of Trays

The town of Tomar in central Portugal is home to one of the most spectacular festivals in the country. The Festival of Trays takes place every two or three years in July outside the local church. The interval between festivals depends on the country's economic situation. In good years, the festival is held frequently; in bad years, more than three years will sometimes pass before another festival takes place.

The Festival of Trays is believed to have pagan origins in an ancient fertility rite dedicated to the goddess Ceres. Officially, however, the festival is associated with Queen Isabel, who founded the Brotherhood of the Holy Spirit in the fourteenth century. Despite her husband's disapproval, Queen Isabel, who later became a saint, frequently hid bread in her dress to give to the poor. One day, when confronted by the king on her way out of the castle, the bread in her apron miraculously turned into roses.

Left: **Young women get help from their escorts to balance trays of bread on their heads during the procession part of the Festival of Trays.**

Above: **Some women manage to balance the trays on their own.**

A Balancing Act

Today, the festival is a secular, highly colorful event, with music, dancing, and fireworks. It is a five-day affair that ends with the procession of trays on the last Sunday of July. Dressed in white, about 400 young women are escorted by young men dressed in white shirts, red ties, and black trousers. The women bear tall trays of bread on their heads. Each tray holds thirty loaves of bread threaded on vertical canes and decorated with colorful leaves and paper flowers. It is topped by a white paper dove, the symbol of the Holy Spirit. The resulting headdress can weigh up to 30 pounds (13.6 kg) and is as tall as its bearer, hence the need for a young man to help balance the tray. The next day, bread, wine, and beef are distributed to the needy, following Queen Isabel's advice to "give bread to the poor."

Music and Dancing

The religious significance of the Festival of Trays is somewhat lost in the exuberant festivities. Throughout the five days, there is music and dancing in the streets. Fireworks are set off at dawn and dusk, and a bullfight takes place the night before the procession of trays.

Foz Côa: Art in Stone

The paintings of Foz Côa were brought to public attention in 1989 when the Electricity Department of Portugal decided to build a large dam near the mouth of the Côa River, a tributary of the Douro. In the course of an environmental study, an important number of archaeological sites were discovered in the river valley over a distance of more than 10 miles (16 km), including four rock shelters with prehistoric paintings.

When the discovery was made public, there were worldwide protests against the construction of the dam. Under the slogan "Petroglyphs can't swim," derived from a popular rap song, high school students from the town of Vila Nova de Foz Côa rallied support from environmentalists and others to make the Portuguese government slow down the construction. By 1995, it became clear that the local population, as well as international opinion, would never accept the dam. In November 1995, the Portuguese government canceled the project and turned the find into the Côa Valley Archaeological Park. Today, the Foz Côa rock art sites are classified as a national monument.

The Foz Côa findings are significant for two reasons. First, this is the largest collection of outdoor Paleolithic figures in the world. Second, Foz Côa is the only known case where rock art

Left: **This Foz Côa rock with a drawing of horses is believed to be more than 10,000 years old. The pre-historic rock artists depicted movement by drawing two or more figures in sequence, much like modern-day cartoon techniques. There is no sign that the Foz Côa artists ever used paint to decorate their drawings; however, since the rock art is outdoors, the paint could have been worn away by the weather.**

from various periods in time, from pre-history to the twentieth century, is found in the same place. The Paleolithic drawings depict aurochs, horses, fish, and ibex. Later engravings of the Post-Paleolithic period show deer and goats. One of the most interesting features of the Foz Côa art is a cluster of modern petroglyphs, which are sometimes signed by the artist. From the seventeenth to the nineteenth centuries, religious motifs, such as large crosses, reliquaries, and monstrances, predominate. Figures from the twentieth century include the sun, moon, and castles.

Above: **Spain's King Juan Carlos (***front, left***) and Portuguese President Jorge Sampaio (***second from left***) investigate the engravings on the walls of the Côa River valley with the help of an archaeologist.**

Fine Techniques

The Paleolithic artists used four main engraving techniques: fine line incision, pecking, abrasion, and scraping. Fine line incision, the easiest technique, is achieved by means of a pointed object drawing lines on the rock face. Pecking is done with the help of a heavy object such as a hammerstone and a chisel. Abrasion consists of wearing away the rock surface inside a figure created by fine line incision or pecking. Scraping is similar to abrasion, but the figure is more extensively abraded, so the resulting contrast between the original surface and the scraped surface brings out the figure.

The Friendly Neighbor?

Portugal's history with Spain has been one of invasion and rebuff. Portucale (Portugal) started out as a small county in the Spanish Kingdom of Leon and Castile in the eleventh century. It became independent of Spanish rule in 1143 when Afonso Henriques was recognized as the country's first king. By the end of the thirteenth century, the Portuguese boundaries were more or less fixed. In 1297, the Treaty of Alcañices was signed, marking Spain's recognition of the frontiers of the Portuguese kingdom. The ruling families of the two countries maintained close links, although the Portuguese nobility was always wary of Spanish intentions. It was fearful of another invasion, and this became a reality in 1373 when Enrique de Trastámara, in order to gain the Spanish throne, invaded Portugal. Twelve years later, the Portuguese rose against the Spanish rulers and the Castilian nobles who had settled in Portugal. In a battle where the odds were firmly stacked against him, João I defeated the Spaniards and restored Portugal to Portuguese rule.

DEU-LA-LEU MARTINS

Popular resentment against the Spaniards is entrenched in the story of Deu-la-leu Martins. In the fourteenth century, Spanish forces besieged the town of Monção. The people were close to starvation, but Deu-la-leu baked some cakes using much skill and next to no flour. She presented these cakes to the enemy who promptly lifted the siege, thinking the town could not fall because of the abundance of food there.

Left: **For the people living on the border with Spain, disputes between the two countries are far from daily life. In the little village of Rio do Onor, for example, nobody pays any notice to the border, which actually runs right through it. The border is marked by a stone with a "P" on one side and an "E" (for España) on the other. People on both sides speak the same dialect, which is neither Spanish nor Portuguese. They have more in common with each other than with the people of Lisbon or Madrid.**

Spanish rule was reestablished in 1580 when King Henrique died without an heir, and Philip II of Spain claimed the throne through his mother, a Portuguese royal princess. Although Philip II was respected by the Portuguese, his successors were viewed with resentment as they used Portugal to raise money and soldiers for Spain's wars overseas. Things came to a head in 1640 when the Spanish rulers tried to recruit Portuguese forces to crush a revolt in Catalonia. The Spaniards were finally forced out of the country in 1668. Portugal has remained independent ever since.

Although the hostility between Portugal and Spain has since subsided, it still flares up now and then because of the proximity of the countries. One example is the "water war" between Portugal and Spain. Many rivers, on which Portugal depends for irrigation and water, have their source in Spain. In 1968, a treaty was signed with Spain to ensure that the waters of the Rio Guadiana, which begins in Spain and flows into the arid Alentejo, were fairly shared. Successive droughts have meant that there is not enough water to go around. Portugal has accused Spain of using more water from the Guadiana than what was agreed, while Spain wants to divert the river to feed its parched south.

Opposite: **Portugal and Spain share a number of rivers. From the mouth of Minho River, Spain is clearly visible.**

Gulbenkian's Legacy

The Calouste Gulbenkian Museum in Lisbon, one of the finest in Portugal, was inaugurated in 1969 to house the art collection bequeathed to the country by one of the wealthiest men of the twentieth century — Calouste Sarkis Gulbenkian. Set in a spacious park, the museum was built to display the thousands of art treasures at their best. Natural light streams into the rooms and allows visitors to appreciate the colors and lines of paintings and sculptures. The museum's star exhibits are Rembrandt's *Portrait of an Old Man* (1645), a marble statue of the Roman goddess Diana (1780) by French sculptor Jean-Antoine Houdon, and a painting of St. Catherine by Flemish artist Rogier Van der Weyden done in the mid-fifteenth century.

Who Was Calouste Gulbenkian?

An Armenian born in Turkey in 1869, Calouste Sarkis Gulbenkian made his fortune from the oil industry. He acted as an intermediary between the United States and the oil-rich Arab

Below: **The Calouste Gulbenkian Museum was built to house and honor Gulbenkian's enviable private collection of art.**

Left: Calouste Sarkis Gulbenkian, considered a recluse by many, never bought a house in Lisbon.

countries. In 1928, he was granted a 5 percent stake in four major oil companies, earning him the nickname "Mr. 5 percent." At times, he was believed to be the richest man in the world. Calouste Gulbenkian took up residence in Portugal during World War II and lived in Lisbon until his death in 1955. Although he adopted Portugal as his country of residence, he never owned a house in the country, preferring to live in a hotel in central Lisbon.

The Gulbenkian Foundation

Upon his death, Calouste Gulbenkian bequeathed his estate, including his priceless art collection, to the Portuguese people in the form of a charitable trust. The foundation, with assets worth more than U.S. $1 billion, concentrates on cultural activities and has its own orchestra, libraries, ballet company, and concert halls. One of the educational projects financed by the foundation is the Calouste Gulbenkian Planetarium in Lisbon. It recreates the night sky and reveals the mysteries of the stars and galaxies.

GULBENKIAN'S TREASURE

Calouste Gulbenkian started collecting art at the age of fourteen when he bought some ancient coins in a bazaar. By the time of his death, his collection had grown to include paintings, vases, murals, and even furniture, spanning over 4,000 years of art. The Gulbenkian collection consists of ancient Egyptian statues, Islamic manuscripts, Chinese jades, Japanese silks, European paintings, French furniture, and Art Nouveau jewelry. One of the most interesting aspects of the collection is the set of Lalique creations. Gulbenkian was a personal friend of French jeweler René Lalique and bought many pieces of jewelry, glassware, and ivory directly from him.

Lisbon

Like Rome, Lisbon is built on seven steep hills. The views from the hilltops take in the whole city, making Lisbon a visually fascinating place. The hills, however, also mean a steep climb from the Baixa (lower town) to the Bairo Alto (upper town). Two *elevadors* (ee-li-va-DORS) — the Elevador da Glória and the Elevador de Santa Justa — move people from one part of the city to another. The former is a bright yellow funicular that rattles up the hill to the Miradouro, the highest point. The other is an elevator built at the beginning of the twentieth century by an apprentice of Gustave Eiffel, the architect of the Eiffel Tower in France. Enclosed within an iron tower, the elevator consists of two cars that travel a vertical distance of 105 feet (32 m).

Lisbon is home to outstanding buildings and museums. The Tower of Belém stands at the mouth of the Tagus as a lone fortress. Built in 1515, it was the last sight of Portugal for ships sailing to explore the world. Nearby is the Jerónimos Monastery, begun in 1501 and financed largely by "pepper money," the riches brought by the spice trade. One of Lisbon's most striking landmarks is the church of Santa Engrácia. The building was started in 1682 but was not completed until 1966, prompting a saying that a Santa Engrácia job was never done. It is now the

Left: **The Tower of Belém was built in 1515 as a fortress. It symbolizes the Portuguese explorations of the world in the fifteenth and sixteenth centuries.**

National Pantheon, housing the tombs of Portuguese heroes such as Vasco da Gama and Luís Vaz de Camões.

Collapse and Reconstruction

On November 1, 1755, a massive earthquake razed Lisbon to the ground. The first tremor was felt at about 9:30 a.m., followed by a second minutes later. It was this second quake that destroyed the city. When it happened, most of the residents were in church celebrating All Saints' Day. Many people were crushed to death when the churches collapsed on them. The candles in the churches also ignited a huge fire that raged for seven days. At about 11 a.m., an enormous tidal wave rolled into town and smashed those buildings that were still standing.

The man entrusted with the rebuilding of the city was the Marquês de Pombal. By the end of November, he had planned a modern grid-like system of roads for the city center. Much of modern-day Lisbon still stands in accordance with Pombal's layout. Lisbon was voted European City of Culture in 1994.

Above: **Situated roughly in the middle of the Portuguese Atlantic coast and built on the northern bank of the Tagus River, Lisbon has been in existence since 1200 B.C. In A.D. 1256, it became the capital of Portugal. Today, Lisbon is a vibrant city and home to people of many nationalities.**

The Lusophone Movement

Nearly 200 million people around the world speak the Portuguese language. Portuguese is the official language of Portugal and its former colonies in South America, Africa, and Asia. Portuguese-speaking countries outside of Portugal include Brazil, Angola, Mozambique, Guinea-Bissau, the Cape Verde Islands, São Tomé e Principe, Macau (a Portuguese colony that was returned to Chinese rule in December 1999), and East Timor (a former Portuguese colony).

In July 1996, the governments of Portugal and the six independent countries of Brazil, Angola, the Cape Verde Islands, Guinea-Bissau, Mozambique, and São Tomé e Principe came together to form the Comunidade dos Países de Língua Portuguesa (CPLP), or the Community of Portuguese-speaking Countries. The CPLP aims to promote Portuguese language and culture, with a secondary objective of strengthening political and diplomatic ties. Economic cooperation is another area in which the CPLP is active.

Former Portuguese Colonies

Among all the former colonies, Brazil remains one of Portugal's most important partners in many areas. Annexed in 1500 by the

Left: **Portuguese soldiers manage a smile during the last days of colonial rule in Angola in 1975.**

Portuguese explorer Pedro Álvares Cabral, Brazil fueled the golden age of Portugal's development. Brazilian gold, tobacco, and sugar filled the coffers of the Portuguese rulers and financed the building of extravagant palaces and splendid churches. In the early nineteenth century, Brazil even became the seat of the Portuguese kingdom when the royal family was forced by the invading French forces to flee Portugal. This led to the colony declaring its independence in 1822. With the loss of Brazil, Portugal entered a period of tumultuous change, culminating in the military revolt of 1926.

Economically, the African colonies were no less important than Brazil for the slaves they supplied to Portugal's slave trade. After the loss of Brazil, Portugal came to rely even more heavily on them for funds. This led to long and costly wars, especially in Mozambique and Angola. It was the disaffection of a group of army officers with the war in Angola that led to the Carnation Revolution of 1974. All African colonies were granted independence in 1975.

In Asia, the small territory of East Timor, upon independence from Portugal in 1975, was violently seized by Indonesia. In 1999, the East Timorese voted overwhelmingly for autonomy. After months of strife and violence, the territory seems set to take its first steps toward independence. Portugal has always stood up for the rights of the East Timorese against Indonesia.

Above and *below:* In 1975, when Indonesia invaded East Timor, the Portuguese showed their anger by cloaking statues in black and putting up banners that cried out against the unlawful act.

Portuguese Islands

The only remnants of the once vast Portuguese empire are the islands of Madeira and the Azores in the Atlantic. Both Madeira and the Azores are autonomous regions, with their own legislatures. Macau, off the coast of China, reverted to Chinese rule in December 1999.

Madeira

Lying about 535 miles (860 km) southwest of Lisbon, the archipelago of Madeira became Portugal's first colony in 1419. Madeira consists of four islands: the fertile Madeira and Porto Santo, and the uninhabited Selvagens and Desertas. The capital is Funchal on Madeira Island. Dotted with cliffs and mountain ranges, lush forests, waterfalls, and flowering plants, Madeira's scenery is breathtaking. Flowering plants at the Botanical Gardens in Funchal include coral trees from Brazil, hibiscus and orchids from Southeast Asia, Cape artichoke from South Africa, and the native Pride of Madeira.

Azores

Located midway between Europe and North America, the nine islands of the Azores became part of Portugal in 1427. The most

Below: **Surrounded by lush vegetation, Funchal, capital of Madeira, lies on the southern coast of the island. With a population of about 120,000, it is home to half the population of the archipelago.**

striking aspect of the Azores is the volcanic origin of the islands. The Azores archipelago emerged from the Atlantic less than 5 million years ago as magma was pushed through faults in the seabed. Today, Pico Alto, the highest peak in the whole of Portugal, on Pico Island is still an active volcano. The island itself is sitting on top of a giant underwater volcano. Remnants of former volcanoes, called calderas, can be seen across the Azores. Calderas are formed when the cone of a volcano collapses during or after an eruption. After the volcano dies, rainwater collects inside the calderas to form crater lakes.

Macau

The oldest permanent European settlement in Asia, Macau became a Portuguese trading post in 1557. Macau consists of two small islands and a peninsula at the mouth of the Pearl River in southern China. Known as the "Las Vegas of the East," Macau boasts seven casinos and two racetracks and holds an annual Grand Prix. Under an agreement made in 1987, Macau was handed back to China in December 1999.

Above: **When Macau (***shown here***) reverted to Chinese rule, it became a special administrative region with an independent capitalist economy. China has granted it the right to remain this way for the next fifty years.**

Wines of Portugal

Portugal produces three main types of wine: vinho verde, Madeira, and port. Vinho verde, produced in the Minho and Douro Litoral provinces, is the most popular wine in Portugal. The name vinho verde, which means green wine, does not refer to the color of the wine but to its crisp, fruity quality. Usually white, vinho verde can also be red. It has a sharp, fresh taste and a slight sparkle brought about by fermentation in the bottle.

Madeira is one of the oldest fortified wines in Portugal. Made on the island of Madeira, it is "cooked" at temperatures of between 104° and 122° Fahrenheit (40° and 50° Centigrade) for six months using the heat of the sun and with the help of hot water pipes. This heating process brings out the taste of the wine. Madeira is then fortified with brandy.

The most well-known Portuguese wine is port. This is a sweet, rich wine made exclusively from grapes grown in the Douro valley. Produced in a strictly limited region of the Upper

Below: **After picking the grapes, harvesters transfer them into a big container. Later, the grapes are crushed.**

Left: Grape crushing is often an occasion for fun and dancing.

Douro, port was "discovered" by the British in the seventeenth century, when British importers turned to Portuguese wines after the import of French wines was prohibited in 1679. To preserve the wine for the journey from Portugal to Britain, two young merchants from Liverpool decided to add some brandy to it so that it would travel better. They found that the resulting wine tasted much better; port was "born." The addition of brandy a couple of days after the grapes are crushed arrests the fermentation, retaining the wine's sweetness and increasing its alcohol content.

How Port Is Made

To make port, grapes are harvested in September and October and then crushed. The juice is left to ferment for two days, after which brandy is added in a ratio of four parts wine to one part brandy. The wine stands in large casks until the following spring, when it is transported to the wine lodges in Oporto. There it remains in oak or chestnut casks for two years, carefully watched and nurtured by tasters. The best wine, called vintage, is bottled and left to mature for about fifteen years before it is deemed fit for drinking. The rest is left in the cask for a few more years before bottling.

Above: Wine tasters are able to test the quality of a wine just by sniffing its aroma.

RELATIONS WITH NORTH AMERICA

The Portuguese did not take part in the early settlement of North America, although Portuguese sailors had visited the United States long before Christopher Columbus "discovered" the North American continent in 1492. Emigration from Portugal to the United States started only in the nineteenth century; since then, Portuguese emigrants have come in a steady stream.

Portugal and North America have usually been on the same side in world politics. Portugal remained neutral during World War II but opened up a base for U.S. and British aircraft on

Below: In July 1997, Portuguese Prime Minister António Guterres welcomed Hillary Clinton at the National Palace in Belem, the first such trip by the wife of a serving U.S. president.

Portuguese soil. Portugal and the United States are founding members of NATO (North Atlantic Treaty Organization), which was established in 1949 to counter the Soviet presence in postwar Eastern Europe. Portugal has always supported the United States in NATO initiatives.

Culturally, Portugal and the United States have drawn benefits from each other. American pop music and fashion are a way of life for Portuguese teenagers, while immigrant communities share some aspects of their Portuguese culture with Americans.

Opposite: Portugal was ranked eighteenth among the world's top tourist destinations in 1997. Most tourists are attracted by the warm weather and sunny beaches of the Algarve, as well as by the mountains of Trás-os-Montes.

Left: **Portuguese explorer Pedro Álvares Cabral sighted Brazil on April 22, 1500.**

Portuguese Explorers in the Americas

Although the Spaniards and the British colonized most of the
Americas, the Portuguese believe they were the first to sight
the continents. The most important Portuguese discovery in the
Americas — Brazil — was made by Pedro Álvares Cabral in 1500.
After he reported his find to the king, the latter sent another
expedition to travel northwestward in search of more land. In
1500, Gaspar Côrte Real landed in Newfoundland and named
it Terra Verde (Green Land), not knowing that John Cabot had
already claimed the land for England in 1476. Real disappeared
a year later when he returned to explore the island. His brother,
Miguel, was dispatched to look for him but he, too, disappeared.

Other explorers of the northeastern coast were João
Fernandes and João Alvares Fagundes. Known as "O lavrador
da Terceira," or the landowner from Terceira, Fernandes gave
his name to the Canadian province of Labrador. Fagundes, a
navigator from Viana do Castelo, explored several islands off
the coast of Newfoundland in the 1520s.

Portuguese adventurers also made their mark on the Western seaboard. João Rodrigues Cabrilho was born in Portugal but lived most of his life in Guatemala. After making his fortune in gold mining, he led a Spanish expedition to explore the northern limits of Spain's colonies in the Americas. Departing from Acapulco in 1542, he sailed as far as the Russian River in California, discovering and naming San Diego Bay and Santa Barbara.

Did the Portuguese "Discover" the Americas?

Despite what American schoolchildren are taught, the Portuguese believe Christopher Columbus was not the first European to set foot in the Americas. An ancient sea chart dating from 1424 lends credence to the view that the land called America today was already known to some Portuguese navigators in the early fifteenth century. This document shows a landmass named "Antilia" across the sea from Europe. Portuguese experts believe that Antilia is America. Amerigo Vespucci, the Italian after whom America is named, learned the art of navigation in Portugal and was in the service of the Portuguese king when he sailed to the Americas in 1499 and 1501.

Below: **The Portuguese are proud to point out that Christopher Columbus (***shown here***) obtained most of his nautical knowledge from the Portuguese. He lived in Portugal for fourteen years, was educated there, married a Portuguese woman from Madeira, and spoke Portuguese.**

Portuguese Settlements in North America

As befitting a nation of seafarers and adventurers, emigration has always been high in Portugal, especially from the Azores and Madeira. A favorite destination is the United States. Since 1957, more Portuguese have migrated to the United States than any other European group. About 300,000 people born in Portugal now live in the United States. Most settlements are concentrated in the New England states and California. Immigration to Canada is more recent, beginning in 1953, when a group of men went to work for the Canadian National Railway. Portuguese communities are present in the provinces of Quebec, Ontario, and British Columbia.

Emigration from Portugal to the United States took place in three phases: 1800–1870, 1870–1920, and after 1957. The first group of emigrants came mainly from the Azores. Emigration increased in the 1830s when a spate of natural disasters fell upon the islands, and the Azoreans faced starvation. Many youngsters joined the whaling ships that stopped over in the Azores for food supplies and to recruit sailors. They later settled in Hawaii, Massachusetts, and California.

Below: **In Fall River, Massachusetts, Portuguese fishermen form the heart of the local community.**

The second wave of emigrants included more people from mainland Portugal. Attracted by better economic prospects in the United States, they were prepared to work hard to succeed. Emigration virtually stopped after 1920 when the American government imposed strict entry conditions. The quota for Azorean emigrants, however, was increased after an underwater volcano erupted in the Azores in 1957, and an earthquake shook the islands in 1964.

Large Portuguese communities are present in Massachusetts and California. On the eastern coast, in the New Bedford area, the early Portuguese settlers entered into familiar occupations, such as fishing, whaling, and textiles. Although Portuguese-Americans are found in all professions now, some of them attend courses at the University of Rhode Island and Cape Cod Technical High School to learn their traditional family crafts. In California, Portuguese settlers initially went into whaling and joined the Gold Rush; later, they settled mainly in the Santa Clara Valley to work on farms. Some of them have moved to Idaho in the last twenty years to join the dairy farming industry. There are now about 4,000 Portuguese-Americans in Idaho.

Above: **The Portuguese community in this Massachusetts countryside keeps alive many of its traditions.**

Prominent Portuguese-Americans

Although the Portuguese community in North America is rather small compared to other European communities, people of Portuguese descent have made their mark on American history, literature, and culture. One of the first Portuguese to distinguish himself as a patriot was Peter Francisco. Serving in the Continental Army, he was later commended for being the "strongest man in the Revolutionary armies." Francisco became a friend of Lafayette, the French nobleman who helped the Americans in the War of Independence, and toured the United States with him in 1824. In 1866, during one of the fiercest wars between the army and native Lakota Indians, John Phillips, who was born in the Azores, became an American hero by riding 236 miles (380 km) in a blizzard to bring help to Fort Kearney's besieged troops.

John Philip Sousa

Known throughout the world as the "March King," John Philip Sousa was born in Washington, D.C., in the mid-nineteenth century. He taught himself the violin and became one of the greatest American composers of all time. After leading the U.S. Marine Band for twelve years, he formed his own band and toured

Left: **John Philip Sousa was born to a poor Portuguese family but made a name for himself later in his life by composing marches.**

the world. In addition to composing more than 140 marches, he also wrote novels and popular songs. One of his most famous marches is *The Stars and Stripes Forever*, which foreigners often associate with the United States. John Philip Sousa composed several operettas and wrote three novels. He took charge of the U.S. Navy band training center during World War I.

John Dos Passos

Born in Chicago in 1896 and educated at Harvard University, John Dos Passos wrote the trilogies *U.S.A.* and *District of Columbia*, as well as several novels on social history and morality. *U.S.A.* is believed to be the closest book to the Great American Novel ever written. A radical leftist in his youth, his political stance shifted to the conservative right in the later part of his life. In his novels, Dos Passos attacked American materialism and hypocrisy between the two world wars. His impressionistic style influenced several generations of American and European novelists.

Traditions of the Portuguese Communities

One of the biggest annual celebrations among Portuguese-Americans is the Holy Ghost Festival. Continuing the tradition of the Holy Spirit celebrations of the Azores, it is celebrated every weekend throughout the summer months. Holy Ghost Organizations work tirelessly to make the celebrations a success. First, they select three "queens": a baby queen, a junior queen, and an adult queen. The queens lead the procession to the church where a special mass is held. After the service, another procession takes the participants to the Holy Ghost Hall, where a free meal of *sopas* (SOH-pas), a thick soup of beef and bread, is served. After the meal, an auction takes place, and proceeds help defray the costs of the celebrations. A small altar is erected in the hall, and the devout go in to pray and make a "promise" to God.

Another tradition is the annual blessing of the boats among the fishing communities in Massachusetts. On the day of the blessing, the fishermen march to the church with banners carrying the names of their boats. After the service, a procession with a statue of Saint Anthony or Saint Peter makes its way to the

Above and *below:* **Portuguese communities in the United States celebrate Camões Day on June 10. Some even dress up as Portuguese explorers for the celebrations.**

pier for the blessing. The boats are cleaned, painted, and decorated with flags and banners. Shop windows are gaily decorated, and everyone takes part in the parties that follow the blessing. The parties tend to be typically American in nature and include cookouts on the beach.

Current Relations: Trade

Relations between the governments of Portugal and the United States center mainly on trade. Although Portugal ranks only thirty-fourth as a market for the export of American goods, the country offers much scope for investment by U.S. firms. Some large American multinational companies have already set up shop in Portugal. They include Ford, Microsoft, Cadence, National Instruments, and United Technologies Automotive. Currently, the United States exports U.S. $1 billion of goods to Portugal. The United States accounts for more than 50 percent of the computer equipment in Portugal and close to 70 percent of the software. American imports of Portuguese goods are not substantial but include cork and textile products.

Below: **The EU flag, which unites the countries of Europe, flies proudly in Lisbon. Portugal is committed to EU policies and is one of the first countries to implement the Euro, the European single currency.**

Cultural Links

Cultural links are strong between Portugal and the United States. The Luso-American Education Foundation was organized by a group of Americans of Portuguese descent. It was founded in 1963 to strengthen the ties between Portugal and the United States and to promote the study of Portuguese language and culture. In 1998, American support for the Lisbon Exposition was one reason for the latter's success. The Americans presented the Portuguese with a memorial wall in the shape of a wave. Called the Luso-American Wave, it is inscribed with the names of Portuguese-Americans who contributed to it.

Fast Foods and Fashion

The big cities in Portugal boast American-style shopping malls and fast food chains. The desire to be "cool" is especially strong among young urbanites, and this includes wearing jeans and leather jackets, eating at fast food joints, and drinking soda pop. The American habit of eating on the run is also catching on among the working population who no longer take two-hour lunch breaks for leisurely meals.

Below: **In cosmopolitan Lisbon, U.S. food chain McDonald's has set up an outlet.**

Music

American music and performers are popular with Portuguese youths. Jazz is played in many Lisbon nightclubs, and the Gulbenkian Foundation organizes the International Jazz Festival every summer. Many American musicians take part in this festival. Those nightclubs playing rock or jazz music have English-sounding names. American audiences, on the other hand, have not been exposed to Portuguese music, although a faint Portuguese sound is heard through the rhythms of Brazilian music.

Movies

Going to the movies is a favorite pastime in Portugal, although most of the movies shown are foreign. Portuguese love American movies, and these are shown in English with subtitles. Portuguese cinema, on the other hand, has suffered greatly from the censorship of the Salazar years. It is only in the last two decades that Portuguese filmmakers have started producing movies in a big way. The Toronto Film Festival showcased Portuguese cinema in 1990, with a retrospective on the films made by Manoel de Oliveira, Portugal's most respected filmmaker.

Above: **Portuguese teenagers are heavily influenced by American clothing styles, donning made-in-U.S.A. jeans and khaki pants.**

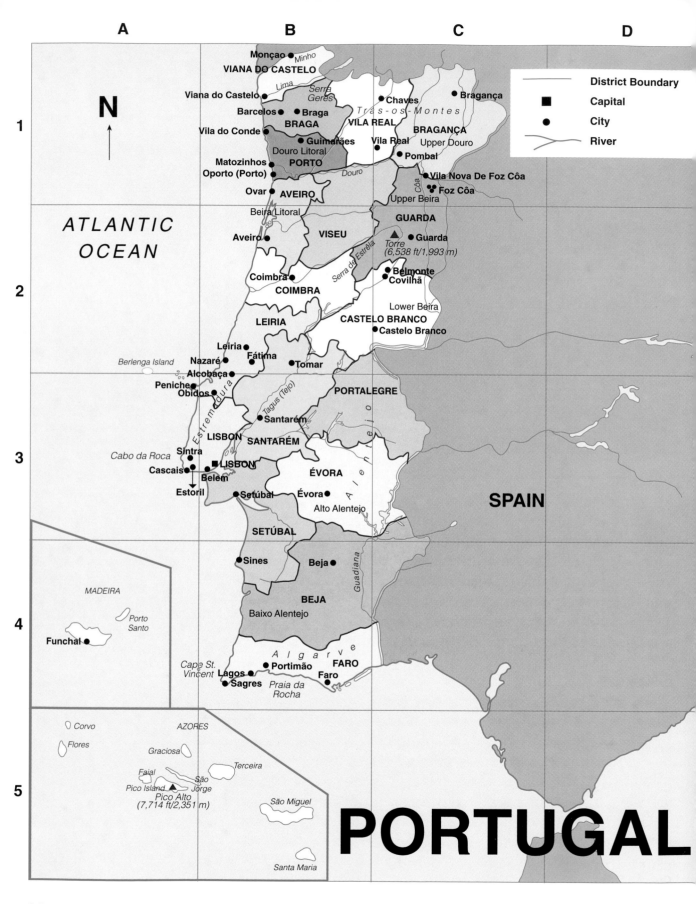

A   B   C   D

District Boundary
■ **Capital**
● **City**
River

Monçao
VIANA DO CASTELO
Minho

Viana do Castelo
Lima
Serra Gerês

Chaves
Bragança

Barcelos   Braga
BRAGA
Trás-os-Montes
VILA REAL
BRAGANÇA

Vila do Conde
Guimarães
Vila Real
Upper Douro

Douro Litoral
PORTO
Pombal

Matozinhos
Oporto (Porto)
Douro
Vila Nova De Foz Côa

Ovar
AVEIRO
Côa   Foz Côa
Upper Beira

N

Beira Litoral
GUARDA

ATLANTIC OCEAN

Aveiro
VISEU
▲ Guarda
Torre (6,538 ft/1,993 m)

Belmonte
Coimbra
Covilhã

COIMBRA
Serra da Estrêla

Lower Beira

LEIRIA
CASTELO BRANCO

Leiria
Castelo Branco

Nazaré   Fátima

Alcobaça
Tomar

Peniche
PORTALEGRE

Obidos
Estremadura

Tagus (Tejo)

Santarém

LISBON
SANTARÉM

Cabo da Roca   Sintra

Cascais   ■**LISBON**
ÉVORA

Belém
Alentejo

Estoril   Setúbal
Évora
SPAIN

Alto Alentejo

SETÚBAL

MADEIRA   *Porto Santo*

Sines   Beja

Guadiana

BEJA

Baixo Alentejo

Funchal

Algarve

Cape St. Vincent
Portimão
FARO

Lagos   Faro
Sagres   *Praia da Rocha*

Corvo   **AZORES**

Flores

Graciosa

Terceira

Faial
São Jorge
Pico Island ▲
Pico Alto (7,714 ft/2,351 m)
São Miguel

PORTUGAL

Santa Maria

86

Above: The Estoril coast in Lisbon has beautiful buildings, both old and new.

Alcobaça B2
Alentejo B3
Algarve B4
Atlantic Ocean A1–A5
Alto Alentejo B3
Aveiro (district) B1
Aveiro B2
Azores A5–B5

Baixo Alentejo B4
Barcelos B1
Beira Litoral B2
Beja (district) B4
Beja B4
Belem B3
Belmonte C2
Berlenga Island A2
Braga (district) B1
Braga B1
Bragança (district) C1
Bragança C1

Cabo da Roca A3
Cape St. Vincent B4
Cascais A3
Castelo Branco (district) B2–C2
Castelo Branco C2
Chaves C1
Côa River C1
Coimbra (district) B2

Coimbra B2
Corvo A5
Covilhã C2

Douro Litoral B1
Douro River B1–C1

Estoril A3
Estremadura A3–B3
Évora (district) B3
Évora B3

Faial A5
Faro (district) B4
Faro B4
Fátima B2
Flores A5
Foz Côa C1
Funchal A4

Graciosa A5
Guadiana River B4
Guarda (district) C1–C2
Guarda C2
Guimarães B1

Lagos B4
Leiria (district) B2
Leiria B2
Lima River B1

Lisbon (district) B3
Lisbon (capital) B3
Lower Beira C2

Madeira A4
Matozinhos B1
Minho River B1
Monçao B1

Nazaré B2

Obidos B3
Oporto (Porto) B1
Ovar B1

Peniche A3
Pico Alto A5
Pico Island A5
Pombal C1
Portalegre (district) B3–C3
Portimão B4
Porto (district) B1
Porto Santo A4
Praia da Rocha B4

Sagres B4
Santa Maria B5
Santarém (district) B3
Santarém B3
São Jorge A5
São Miguel B5
Serra de Estrela B2
Serra Geres B1
Sines B4
Sintra A3
Setúbal (district) B3
Setúbal B3
Spain C1–D5

Tagus (Tejo) River B3
Terceira B5
Tomar B2
Torre C2
Trás-os-Montes B1–C1

Upper Beira C1
Upper Douro C1

Viana do Castelo (district) B1
Viana do Castelo B1
Vila do Conde B1
Vila Nova de Foz Côa C1
Vila Real (district) B1–C1
Vila Real C1
Viseu (district) B2

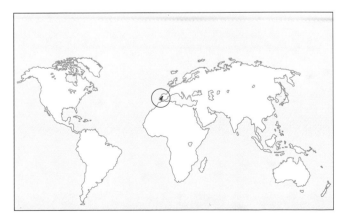

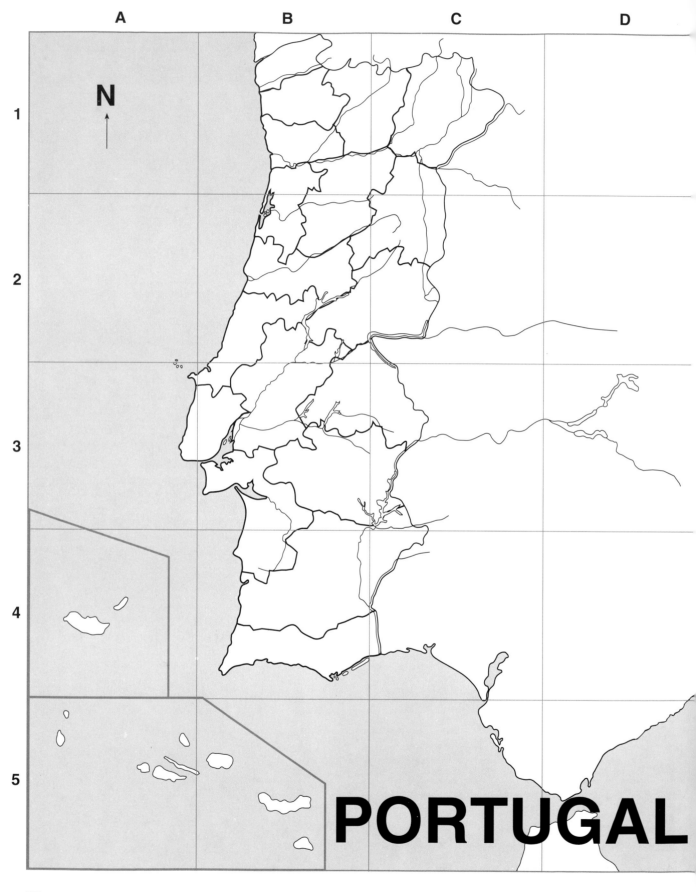

How Is Your Geography?

Learning to identify the main geographical areas and points of a country can be challenging. Although it may seem difficult at first to memorize the locations and spellings of major cities or the names of mountain ranges, rivers, deserts, lakes, and other prominent physical features, the end result of this effort can be very rewarding. Places you previously did not know existed will suddenly come to life when referred to in world news, whether in newspapers, television reports, or other books and reference sources. This knowledge will make you feel a bit closer to the rest of the world, with its fascinating variety of cultures and physical geography.

Used in a classroom setting, the instructor can make duplicates of this map using a copy machine. (PLEASE DO NOT WRITE IN THIS BOOK!) Students can then fill in any requested information on their individual map copies. Used one-on-one, the student can also make copies of the map on a copy machine and use them as a study tool. The student can practice identifying place names and geographical features on his or her own.

Above: **Nature lovers admire a grotto on Pico Island.**

Portugal at a Glance

Official Name	The Republic of Portugal
Capital	Lisbon
Official Language	Portuguese
Population	10 million
Land Area	35,672 square miles (92,390 square kilometers)
Districts	Aveiro, Beja, Braga, Bragança, Castelo Branco, Coimbra, Évora, Faro, Guarda, Leiria, Lisbon, Porto, Portalegre, Santarém, Setúbal, Viana Do Castelo, Vila Real, Viseu
Highest Point	Torre (6,538 feet/1,993 m), Serra de Estrela region in mainland Portugal
Longest River	Tagus
National Emblem	Cockerel
Main Religion	Roman Catholicism
Major Festivals	New Year (January), Carnival (February), Easter (March/April), Fátima Pilgrimage (May & October), Holy Spirit (May), Corpus Christi (June), Festival of Trays (July), Our Lady of Sorrows (August), All Saints' Day (November), Immaculate Conception (December), Christmas (December)
Anniversaries	Carnation Revolution (April 25), Labor Day (May 1), Camões Day (June 10), Republic Day (October 5), Independence Day (December 1)
Famous Explorers	Bartholomeu Diaz (1450–1500), Pedro Álvares Cabral (born c.1460), Vasco da Gama (1460–1524), Ferdinand Magellan (1480–1521)
Currency	Escudos (190$86 escudos = U.S. $1 as of January 2000)

Opposite: **Colorful cockerels are the national emblem of Portugal.**

Glossary

Portuguese Vocabulary

azulejos (ah-zoo-LAY-shoss): ceramic tiles in bright colors.

bacalhau (bah-kahl-O): dried salted codfish, a staple ingredient in Portuguese cooking.

bolo rei (boh-lo RAY): a type of doughnut eaten during Christmas.

caldo verde (KAL-do VEHR-duh): a green-colored soup made from cabbage, potatoes, and smoked sausage.

cataplana (ka-ta-PLAN-na): a copper pan in the shape of a clam in which food is cooked and served.

cavaleiro (ka-val-EY-roh): a bullfighter mounted on a horse.

cavaquinho (ka-va-KEEN-noh): a four-stringed instrument accompanying fado.

centavo (sen-TAH-voh): the one hundredth part of the monetary unit of Portugal.

conto (KON-toh): one thousand escudos.

elevador (ee-li-va-DORS): cable car or elevator.

escudo (ess-KOO-doh): the monetary unit of Portugal that is equivalent to one hundred centavos.

fado (FAH-doh): a bluesy type of song that has become part of Portuguese national culture.

guitarra portuguesa (gi-TAR-rah por-tu-GEH-sah): a twelve-stringed guitar accompanying fado.

latifúndios (lah-tee-FOON-dee-ohs): large agricultural estates.

romaria (roh-mah-ree-AH): a religious festival honoring a saint.

saudade (sow-DAH-de): a deep nostalgia for things past; best expressed in fado songs.

vinho verde (VEE-nyo VEHR-duh): a young wine produced in the Minho and Douro provinces.

English Vocabulary

archipelago: a chain of islands.

arid: being very dry and not having enough rainfall to support plant life.

armillary sphere: a navigational device used by sailors of olden times to measure the positions of the stars.

auroch: the wild ancestor of today's cattle.

autonomous: self-governing.

aversion: a great dislike for someone or something.

basilica: a huge church with a nave.

benefactor: a person who helps another person or an organization by giving money or other items of value.

caldera: a crater formed when the cone of a volcano collapses.

caravels: small sailing ships used by Portuguese explorers.

CPLP (Comunidade dos Países de Língua Portuguesa): an organization of Portuguese-speaking countries formed in 1966 to promote Portuguese language and culture and strengthen member countries' political and diplomatic ties.

detrimental: harmful.

dinghy: a small boat.

dissolution: the official break-up or termination of an organization or institution.

dressage: the performance of special movements by a trained horse.

European Union (EU): an economic and political organization, established in 1993, including most of the states of Western Europe.

expedition: a long journey with a specific purpose, such as exploration.

facade: the front wall or any wall of a building that is given special architectural treatment.

funicular: a cable car.

gargantuan: huge; a great amount.

grotto: a small cave, such as those found on Berlenga Island.

heyday: a period of time marked by great success or accomplishments.

homage: respect.

homogeneous: describes members of a group who are essentially alike.

ibex: a wild goat.

legacy: anything handed down from the past; for example, from an ancestor, predecessor, or from a foreign power's rule over a country.

lucrative: profitable.

majolica: glazed earthenware that is usually richly decorated.

Manueline: an ornate, nautical style of architecture inspired by Portuguese sailing and the exploration of lands in different parts of the world.

monarchy: a government in which a king or queen reigns over a country or empire.

monstrances: symbolic representations of God, in the Catholic Church, which look like the sun with rays emanating from it.

Moors: Berber Muslim invaders from North Africa who left an indelible mark on Portugal.

penitence: heartfelt remorse for a mistake or wrongdoing.

persecution: cruel and unfair treatment of a person or group of people.

petroglyph: a drawing made in stone.

pilgrim: a person who makes a long journey to a sacred religious site as an act of devotion.

poignant: very sad; deeply affecting a person's feelings.

port: a sweet, rich wine made exclusively from grapes grown in the Douro valley, Portugal, and fortified by the addition of grape brandy.

prolific: productive; marked by abundant productivity.

prow: the front part of a boat or ship.

ravaged: completely destroyed.

reconquest: the movement during the Middle Ages in Portugal to take back the land seized by the Moors.

socialism: an economic and social system in which a country's major industries are owned by the state.

Spanish Inquisition: a judicial system instituted in Spain in the fifteenth and sixteenth centuries that persecuted non-Catholics and other heretics.

transhumance: the seasonal migration of people and their livestock between two regions.

troubadour: a French court poet.

More Books to Read

The Explorer's Handbook: How to Become an Intrepid Voyager. Marilyn Tolhurst (Dutton Books)

Ferdinand Magellan. Explorers of the New World series. Jim Gallagher (Chelsea House)

The Food of Portugal. Jean Anderson (William Morrow & Co.)

The Lusiads. World's Classics series. Luís Vaz de Camões (Oxford University Press)

Magellan and da Gama: To the Far East and Beyond. Beyond the Horizons series. Clint Twist (Raintree/Steck Vaughn)

Magellan: A Voyage Around the World. Fiona MacDonald (Franklin Watts)

New Life in an Old Village: A Family in Portugal. Families of the World series. Helene Tramblay (Peguis)

Portugal. Major World Nations series. Ronald Seth (Chelsea House)

Portugal. Modern Industrial World series. Neil Champion (Thomson Learning)

Portugal in Pictures. Visual Geography series. James Nach (Lerner)

Videos

Portugal. (Camera One)

Portugal. The Land of Discoveries. (Ivn Entertainment)

Portugal: Southern Coast & Lisbon. (Questar)

Web Sites

www.portugal.com

www.the-news.net

www.portugal.org

www.madeira-island.com

port-wine.com/uk/index.html

Due to the dynamic nature of the Internet, some web sites stay current longer than others. To find additional web sites, use a reliable search engine with one or more of the following keywords to help you locate information on Portugal: *Age of Discoveries, Azores and Madeira, Eusebio, fado, Fatíma, Portuguese history, wines of Portugal.*

Index